LIVING WELL
LATER IN LIFE

*Emotional and Social Preparation
for RETIREMENT*

*How To Answer the Question:
"WHEN SHOULD I RETIRE?"
The "Gift" of Changing and Aging*

Michael Townshend

authorHOUSE®

AuthorHouse™
1663 Liberty Drive
Bloomington, IN 47403
www.authorhouse.com
Phone: 1 (800) 839-8640

Published by AuthorHouse 06/19/2017

ISBN: 978-1-5246-9671-9 (sc)
ISBN: 978-1-5246-9670-2 (hc)
ISBN: 978-1-5246-9669-6 (e)

Library of Congress Control Number: 2017909344

Print information available on the last page.

Any people depicted in stock imagery provided by Thinkstock are models, and such images are being used for illustrative purposes only. Certain stock imagery © Thinkstock.

This book is printed on acid-free paper.

Because of the dynamic nature of the Internet, any web addresses or links contained in this book may have changed since publication and may no longer be valid. The views expressed in this work are solely those of the author and do not necessarily reflect the views of the publisher, and the publisher hereby disclaims any responsibility for them.

CONTENTS

PART THREE
GROWING OLDER –
GRACEFULLY (JOYFULLY)

PART FOUR
DECISIONS REGARDING RETIREMENT
FULLY PREPARING OURSELVES
EMOTIONALLY AND SOCIALLY
(BEYOND FINANCIAL PLANNING)

PREFACE

LIVING WELL LATER IN LIFE

Emotional and Social Preparation for Retirement

THERE ARE SO many books and informational resources on the topic of Retirement, already. Most of them, you'll note, address the many financial considerations, strategies, laws, budget forecasting, investments, and the like. To convince yourself of this, just google the word, "Retirement" and you will be presented with pages and pages of references and web sites. You will see that easily 99% of the citations regard financial issues and assistance being offered in these matters.

Now, to be sure, this is a very important aspect of the Retirement calculation and decision. Oh, sure. If we don't have enough resources in terms of income and assets, Retirement will be very problematic. So, I applaud the many resources that are available to manage the financial aspect of the Retirement decision. I used many them myself.

This book intends to describe, in plain language, the emotional impact of *CHANGE* in general and specifically addresses the fears and challenges faced by those experiencing changes and transitions in their career, those who are over age 50 who are endeavoring to be relevant in the workforce, as well as preparing themselves for transition into their retirement years.

I draw on more than thirty years of experience, working with people who are experiencing radical change in their lives, primarily in their workplace.

I have been told that I am in a unique position to assist people who are undergoing Change during highly traumatic times. I will endeavor to show you, the reader, ways to find the "promise" and the "opportunity" that lies just beneath the surface as we advance in age both within the world of work and as we prepare ourselves emotionally for retirement.

This book describes simple approaches to help the reader see his or her situation in a new light and discover promising options for a bright future.

In the chapters ahead, I will provide tried and true methods to help you change the way you respond to challenging changes in the workplace and how to assess your emotional and social readiness for the Retirement leg of your life's journey. You will learn how to take charge of your life rather than merely reacting to whatever comes your way.

I hope that this book will lift the spirits of even the most fearful reader.

Anyone facing sleepless nights, wondering what the future holds will find solace in these pages, recognizing, for instance, that anxiety is common and "normal."

The reader will be given concrete steps that have helped thousands of people to overcome these same fears, allowing them to uncover their greatest potential and to be successful, even during the most difficult of times.

This book is a "must read" for anyone who is over age 50 and still working. It will help with the many decisions about how to be the most successful at work during this time in our lives, and give a step-by-step approach to the non-financial aspects of preparing for a wonderful retirement. This is a book to be read again and again.

ACKNOWLEDGEMENTS

THROUGHOUT THIS BOOK I share what I have learned from the thousands of people with whom it has been my privilege to work over the past thirty-five years. They have inspired me immensely while I have helped them through tough periods of change.

The work that I have done has always been organizationally sponsored. That is to say, companies and government agencies have engaged my services through several consulting firms to assist their employees to be successful during times of organizational and personal change.

So, this would be an ideal point at which to sincerely thank those sponsors. Without their humanity, the work that I do could not take place. It takes a lot of courage to see beyond the purely measurable Returns on Investments – to spend capital on services in which the results are difficult to calculate. But these insightful executives have seen past the immediate promise of loss or gain. They have recognized that people want to succeed, but at certain times need some help to find their way. It has been tremendously rewarding for me to function in that capacity.

Additionally, I have been helped enormously by the wisdom and practice of Buddhism, a faith that has taught me to see the intrinsic humanity in all my clients and life associates. By believing in the profound potential in every individual, I have allowed myself to look past their fears and frailties to see dignity and promise. Few are aware of their full potential to achieve profound happiness and to contribute to society. It has been a tremendous privilege to hold up a mirror of the soul for so many, enabling them to discover their hidden capabilities and talents.

I extend my deep appreciation to the following people for their help and advice:

- Daisaku Ikeda, a twenty first century Buddhist Philosopher who taught me to value compassion and dialogue as the keys to living the most meaningful life thus gaining the greatest treasure of all – the treasure of the heart.
- My graduate school professors: Carole Lyles, Charlie and Edie Seashore, and Michael Broom, who taught me to hear the hearts of others and give voice to my own.
- My colleague, Richard Bolles, author of the book, *What Color Is Your Parachute?* who challenged me to complete my books for the sake of others.

INTRODUCTION

THIS BOOK REPRESENTS my research and realizations regarding the process of aging – it's challenges and inherent joys. These are real and identifiable experiences that I have observed in so many folks, and in my own growing journey. I am, at this writing, fast approaching my 70th birthday and I am deeply determined to find the joy in every day and every experience along the way.

Every day of my life presents new challenges (things on my body and in my mind, that do not work like they used to – sometimes they don't work at all and sometimes they work when they're not supposed to) and I am determined to see the humor in every turn of events. This seems crucial to me.

Well, I, like everyone else, have a choice. I can see the changes in my body and mind as terrible curses and begrudge them.

Oh, when I resided at an independent living community, I met several fellow seniors who expressed their sadness at growing older – I know those folks are out there and, of course I understand how they feel this way.

But for me, I just will not go down this road.

You see, how each of us responds to this turn of events in life (aging) is a choice that we make – consciously or otherwise.

And I have made the choice to see all changes as simply, "part of the deal" when growing older. In fact, I can barely contain my joy knowing that I have lived this long. So many that I have loved did not.

So, I find myself, in these years, spending time appreciating my life – just as it is. I see it (aging) as neither good nor bad, right nor wrong. It just is.

My challenge is to continue to live my life enjoying each day. Yes, this is a full out sport that requires conditioning and thoughtfulness. In this book, I will share with the reader the observations and reasoning that have allowed me the immense pleasure to be and to be happy. Now, THAT is an arrival that is worth reading someone's book to learn. Yes?

In these pages, I wish for each reader the "AHA" that will encourage you to not only read on, but to find your compass, your spirit. And please take bold steps during this latter part of your life's journey and join me in saying, on our very last day:

"Wow. That was a GREAT life – a GREAT RIDE. How magnificent. I think that I will go to sleep now and get ready to do this all again. Fantastic!"

PART ONE

••

Living Well During Times Of Change

The NATURE of Life: Change and Transition

LIVING WELL - INTRODUCTION

I AM SURE that we all are aware that change has been woven into the fabric of every aspect of each of our lives. It has been inevitable and ever-present.

Think back over the years of our life. Yes, since birth, things have just not stayed the same at any juncture.

For example, even the experience of birth was the experience of change, even though we didn't recognize it as such at the time (we were a bit pre-occupied). Yes, we came from the warm and wet, fully nourishing environment of our mother's womb into a world that was loud and confusing and we, for the first time, had to work at survival – by breathing.

This was quite a change. But it got progressively more confusing.

Before long, we were taken out of the sterile white rooms, wrapped very tightly in a blanket, and put into a vehicle for a ride to a mysterious new place that we would one day come to know as "home".

Also, we were surrounded by people for the first time both at the hospital and now at home. This was very new for us, but we would get used to it, as there wasn't much of a choice. And, eventually, we would come to be comforted by the presence of others, especially the one with the bosoms full of milk. Yes, we would get used to that very quickly.

We would spend the next five years, or so, in this ever more comfortable environment and, for most, come to like it very much. During this time, we would learn to communicate with the others who surrounded us and that would make things more comfortable, for the most part.

And then, one fine day, we would be taken to a brand-new environment where lots of people our own age would surround us and we would have a whole new challenge in getting to understand how to make the most of this new deal.

Over the next ten years, or so, we grew along with our new friends and playmates and, usually, grew competent at the business of interacting and understanding the many differences of those around us.

In time, we left the High School years and, many of us, went on to college. And this change was BIG.

Let me stop this litany of growth and change for a moment to point out that each stage of change comes with a common element.

When we left our family, to go into college, or into the military, or to take a job living on our own, or met our forever love and decided to marry, or to purchase our first home: in all of this, we ran smack into the quirky reality of change.

You see, every single change in our lives whether what I've noted so far, and/or the many life changes to come including aging, work promotions, new jobs, sickness, and deterioration – well these changes have had **one common denominator**, *FEAR*.

That's right. Whether we acknowledged its presence or not, we had a moment (or many moments) when we questioned ourselves about our pending change. It frightened us. All of us. And always this has been the case.

In *The Crack-Up*, F. Scott Fitzgerald penned his famous line, "In a real dark night of the soul it is always three o'clock in the morning".

This sums it up for me. Each of us has experienced the *devil of doubt*. It is easy to understand. I am sure that the fear that we experience just before a change in our lives can be attributed to the fear of moving from the Known to the Unknown.

But, I know that we all have experienced this, for some, more profoundly that for others.

The way that this fear has manifested itself has often come as a surprise to us. Here is how it often happens: Let's say we have selected a college to attend that we have always wanted on our resume and to which we are ecstatic to be accepted. HOORAY!

But, no matter how many high-fives we have shared over this with family, friends, and teachers, and no matter how much we have dreamed about this new experience, just around the corner; and, no matter how much we have bragged that this is the very best thing that has ever happened – for each of us in this situation, there has come a moment of doubt, either immediately before leaving home to claim our dorm room, or, often, on the very first night in our new university lounge, when we find ourselves alone. Somewhere in this time frame, we have stopped and questioned ourselves, silently, "What have I done?" "Is this the best thing for me?" "Have I made a grave mistake?"

Yes, we have asked these questions to the universe, kept them to ourselves, and have been delighted to learn (some weeks or months later) that all is well and this change really HAS been for the best.

This phenomenon plays out for new relationships, as well as for decisions to marry, even with the truest love of our lives. All of us, in the quiet of our soul, has doubted or at least questioned our sanity at the very last minute (or, many times, within the first 48 hours of the new marriage, partnership, job, and so forth).

An example that clearly shows this phenomenon at work is this, from my own life.

The very first home that I bought was in Greenbelt, Maryland. I was able, for the first time, to use my military service benefit of a Veterans Affairs Home Loan Guarantee and it would prove to be a relatively simple matter.

To make this even easier, I was buying the home with my best friend as a co-owner.

To find the right home, we spent time describing our wants and needs in a house. We came to agreements on location, size, costs, and so forth and shared all of this with a professional realtor who we trusted.

Well, the realtor could find the perfect home that met all of the wants and needs for both of us. It was priced just right and came with a one-year guarantee. We were delighted.

So, we wrote and signed an offer and our realtor promised to call us later that evening to let us know the status of the deal.

We were eating dinner at my apartment that evening when the phone rang. It was our agent calling to tell us that the offer had been accepted with no changes. She even gave us the closing date for the property settlement.

Well, we couldn't be more excited. We took turns calling our folks to tell them the good news (our parents were each putting up a portion of the closing costs, as I recall).

I had a saved bottle of Champaign in my refrigerator and we broke it out and finished it off in celebration with lots of high-fives and dreams of a new life for each of us – now as homeowners.

Later that night, however, I found myself unable to sleep, just sitting on the side of my bed with many conflicting thoughts.

At just that time, my phone rang and it was my friend who had gone back to his home a few hours before. While apologizing for calling so late, I stopped him and said, "I'm wide awake and I can't stop wondering if we're getting into this house a little too quickly". My friend said, "Wow. I was calling to ask, '<u>What</u> have we <u>done</u>?'"

Yes, we both were having immediate doubts and we were both embarrassed but admitted to this consternation.

Well, we went through with the purchase (legally, we didn't have much choice). The experience worked out just fine for both of us. He met the girl who lived next door to the new house and the two of them have been happily married for many years – now enjoying their grandchildren.

We owned the home together for a little over three years at which point he and his fiancé bought out my interest and lived, well, happily ever after – as I said above.

But, note the principle here. The fear was quite natural. I'm quite sure that it is universal. I might even go so far as to say that the Universe has inserted this principle into the mix of *change* to ensure that we common mortals will give changes their full due consideration and not take *change* lightly, even though it is inevitable.

And, now to the meat of my thinking on this topic.

Yes, change is ever-present and, to be sure, it is a scary thing.

But, a life well lived, I think, is a life that manages changes and the fears that change promotes and finds the joy in the process, no matter what. Happiness, joy, even zest would describe the type of life filler that I am determined to find and enjoy, all day, every day. And this is very close at hand for me and for you, the reader. Let me spend a few pages now to describe how to find this joy, this Life Well Lived.

CHAPTER 1

What is "Living Well"?

A life well lived is one that is lived powerfully and is characterized, at a minimum, by the following:
- ☐ **Happiness**
- ☐ **Harmonious Relationships**
- ☐ **Self-Assurance**
- ☐ **Absence of Regrets**
- ☐ **Wisdom**
- ☐ **Zest for Living**

WHEN SOMETHING HAPPENS unexpectedly, something that alters our lives inexorably, it is easy to feel like we are helpless victims of our circumstances, that life has dealt us a fatal blow.

As we make our way through life we invariably experience a wide variety of changes such as: the loss of a job, the termination of a committed relationship, the death of a loved one, debilitating illness, the many challenges of growing older physically, and the like. Traumatic change can leave us feeling we are in a no-win situation, that there is no way to escape the feeling of doom.

It is at times like these, when it is easy to lose hope, we are most likely to feel powerless. All too often, we mistakenly consider that our value as a person is determined by outside factors such as our job, our youth, or our relationship with a loved one.

Over the course of my career, counseling thousands of people undergoing stressful and unsettling Change, I have witnessed a multitude of scenarios for coping with unwelcome new circumstances.

I have concluded that **the way in which someone** *responds* at a crucial time is quite critical, as there is a clear cause-and-effect relationship between an individual's reaction to Change and the eventual outcome reached (both quantitatively and qualitatively).

I would like to share some common-sense strategies that have proved to be useful, as we grow older. These include techniques for self-improvement and useful exercises for the body, the mind, and the spirit that, when practiced over a period of time every day, will enable those of us in transition (that would be all of us) to meet the challenges ahead in an effective and fulfilling way– ultimately resulting in greater self-awareness, accomplishment, and happiness.

Indeed, the overwhelming majority of clients that I have counseled over the years have successfully navigated their way through even the most turbulent times. In fact, their improved circumstances ended up being in stark contrast to their initial circumstances and reaction, when they had anticipated the worst conclusion imaginable. In the end, most have gained, not lost.

What is Living Well?

Living Well is an approach to life that allows us to *take charge* of our circumstances, to recognize the inevitable good that will arise from any series of events and to make of the most of any change, every day.

A life well lived is one that is lived <u>purposefully</u> and <u>memorably</u> and is characterized by, at a minimum, the following:

- A general, unshakeable feeling of **Happiness**
- Consistently **Harmonious Relationships**
- High level of **Self-Assurance**
- An absolute **Absence of Regrets**
- A reliable presence of **Wisdom**
- A **Zest for Living** that can be recognized by others

I now know that the **potential** for all the above conditions resides within each of us. These are not characteristics we need to *develop* but rather, qualities to *discover*, qualities that lie dormant in each of us. While these attributes may be buried deep within, nonetheless, they exist– like diamonds in a mine, waiting to be excavated.

Let me share with you a parable from the most profound Buddhist teaching called *The Lotus Sutra*. The story is called "The Hidden Jewel."

A STORY- The Hidden Jewel

A wealthy man was traveling on a long journey. He was very tired and lonely at the end of several days of difficult travel. As evening approached, he saw a man on the side of the road who had set up camp for the night and who was roasting a large rabbit over a fire.

The wealthy man approached the stranger and asked if he could share the warmth of the fire. He was delighted to find that the stranger welcomed his company and generously offered to share his feast and his tent for the night. The stranger seemed to go out of his way to be generous with him and to talk congenially into the late evening after the delicious meal.

The stranger said that he was not on a journey but that he had experienced some misfortunes and was without a home. Still, he was cheerfully willing to share what he had and enjoyed the company of anyone who happened along.

The wealthy man offered to assist the stranger but found that the stranger was a proud person who preferred not to accept handouts. He expressed deep gratitude to the wealthy man for his offer and suggested that they turn in.

The wealthy man was the first to awake the next morning. He sincerely desired to assist this new friend but did not want to embarrass him by trying again to give him money.

Instead, the wealthy man took a precious jewel from his purse that was extremely valuable, worth well beyond the financial needs of most people over a lifetime. He quietly sewed the jewel into the lining of the stranger's cloak, assuming that by the time the stranger discovered the jewel, the wealthy man would be long gone and, thus, embarrassment would be avoided. He returned to his journey shortly after the stranger awoke and after he had profusely thanked the stranger for his assistance and friendship.

Over the next ten years, the stranger continued to wander, suffering greatly from the winters and regular scarcity of food.

One day when the stranger was lying by the side of the road and suffering the pain of hunger and cold, the wealthy man happened along once again. Finding his friend in this condition, he immediately carried him to the nearest town for shelter and food. He stayed with him for several days until the stranger's health had sufficiently improved.

Recognizing the wealthy man, the stranger thanked him for his help and told him that he had rethought his previous prideful refusal of help and felt that he should have accepted his friend's generosity.

At this point, the wealthy man asked him what had become of the jewel. The stranger said that he didn't know of any jewel. So, the wealthy man searched the cloak and found that it was still in the lining just as he had left it.

The Moral

We all possess a "hidden jewel" that many of us have yet to discover. This precious jewel holds the promise of unimaginable happiness because it represents the profound wisdom and vast potential intrinsic in each of us. Once we realize that this inherent treasure exists, deep within our life, we recognize we have the power to take control and determine our own destiny. The challenge becomes to learn how to detect and then fully utilize this tremendous good fortune that we all possess.

By adopting an optimistic perspective, the unlimited resources at our disposal become more and more apparent. We find our past experiences of overcoming obstacles, our ability to practice patience and perseverance, our sense of humor and appreciation and our indomitable spirit to always progress - these combine to create a diamond-like life that can withstand anything, and that shines for all time.

A Story – Never Give Up

My friend studied hard for the Certified Public Accountant (CPA) exam. But despite his efforts, he failed the exam numerous times, exasperatingly sometimes just by one or two points. But he just kept taking it, over and over every time it was offered. He wouldn't give up.

Although he studied very hard for each examination, he just kept missing in one area or another. I used to worry that his frustration would shake his naturally positive personality. But he just kept trying, and was determined never to feel embarrassed.

What a spirit! He understood something very important. Happiness in life is not just about outcomes. Our attitude to enjoy the journey is what counts. "Winning" and "losing" are artificial measures. How often does a "win" turn out to be a "loss," and vice versa?

He never felt ashamed because he did not define himself by the outcome. Rather, he came to enjoy his persona as the guy who never stopped trying. Even though he felt awkward when he received his grades, his friends and family deeply admired him and were inspired immensely. My friend? Well he just kept trying and finally passed. He was promoted to a top financial position at a Fortune 500 company. His bosses have re-named him "Relentless."

Most importantly, he now knows he can accomplish whatever goal he sets– and enjoy every step of the way.

CHAPTER 2

The Cycle of Emotions: Recognizing and Managing Emotions During Change

☐ Expect Waves of Emotions
☐ Prepare for Awkwardness and Ambiguity
☐ Rely on Patience and Curiosity

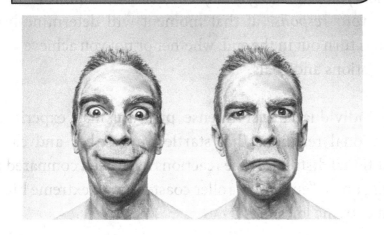

LIFE *IS* CHANGE. Life is a series of challenges. Some of the changes and challenges we face turn out well. Some don't. What I have learned –both in business and any other aspect of life– is that what matters is how a person *reacts* to these challenges, and CHANGE.

When a drastic, unexpected, or unwanted Change occurs in our business or private lives – whether it is the loss of a job, a merger, or a downsizing, or a personal loss, the loss of a partner – the vast proportion of us tend to react rashly, creating the potential for negative consequences in the future. When our prosperity and well-being hinge on our response, we don't want the outcome to be one of regret, thinking to ourselves, "If only I hadn't said that." "If only I hadn't done that." "If only I had known, then things would have turned out better." We don't want to look back and have to say, "Hindsight is 20/20."

When you are facing a major transition, remind yourself that *your response* at that moment will determine how things turn out in the end, whether or not you achieve your aspirations and goals.

An individual under intense pressure may experience emotional reactions that startle him or her and cause additional distress. These reactions have been compared to being on an "emotional roller coaster," with extreme highs and extreme lows.

The Cycle of Emotions

The noted psychologist, Dr. Elisabeth Kubler-Ross, in her hallmark study, *On Death and Dying,* was the first researcher to identify and describe in vivid detail the cycle of emotions that many of us experience when facing far-reaching changes in our lives. She called them "Stages of Grief."

Any one of us may experience any or all of these stages when under extreme stress or suffering a loss. I find it useful to identify these stages, to prepare for these feelings, and to manage them. Please remember: these reactions are entirely Normal.

Take comfort in the fact that **YOU ARE NOT UNIQUE** and **YOU ARE NOT ALONE**.

Recognizing the stages that are common to the human condition will help you to:

- Prepare yourself for awkwardness and ambiguity in the face of change.
- Guide yourself in these times with Patience and Curiosity.

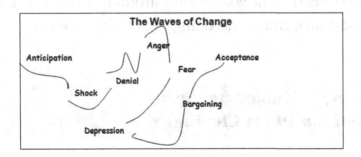

I call these "waves" or "stages" of change and point them out here because they are applicable to any situation where trauma, loss, or unwanted Change is occurring.

Examining these stages of emotional reactions will provide insight into the grieving process so that, when you experience loss you won't be stunned by what you are feeling. You will be able to acknowledge that this experience is necessary as a first step in recovering and moving forward toward a bright future.

Anticipation

In most of the experiences that have been shared with me about the workplace over the years, the fact that Change was brewing or that a Change had occurred was just NOT a surprise. Not at all.

Most people receive a warning sign of some sort. I'll bet that you did, too. This is not to say that you really knew for sure, but you probably had a hunch that something was up. Perhaps you were hearing the gossip going around, or you might have noticed management was doing something different.

A Story – Rumormongers Predict a Plant Closing

I was called in to help with a plant closing in the Midwest some years ago. I arrived the week prior to the announcement of the closing to the employees. Everything seemed "hush-hush." Only the plant's most senior managers and Human Resources staff had been told that the company's headquarters had decided to close this plant. They asked me to consult to the management to minimize the likelihood of violence and negative local press.

In our first meeting, one of the managers commented that the "secrecy pact" was working quite well. They were sure that no one in the plant knew of the impending closure. I was quick to point out, however, that if this was not already the subject of rumor and mounting anxiety, this would be a first in my experience. I cautioned the management to be aware of signs of stress at all levels (including among themselves) and to move ahead without delay.

Several days later, a meeting of all employees was called with only a minimum of notice. As the employees filed into the makeshift auditorium, I sat in the back row and listened carefully. I knew that I'd be able to gauge the crowd's collective emotions and, thus, be more helpful to the entire group with that knowledge.

As employees entered the room, I heard phrases like "Well, this is it!" "I told you it would happen this week!" "I wonder how long they'll keep my shift running," and so forth.

I was not surprised in the least. As always, people in the plant had read signals and had judged the demeanor of management to easily surmise the state of affairs.

The employees of that plant had noticed the decreasing level of incoming orders as well as managers' reluctance to reorder component stock and simple supplies.

Most telling of all were three requests for employment verification related to mortgage applications, which were being "sat on" by Human Resources for more than a week. This delay was highly unusual and the word had spread like wildfire through the plant.

Rumormongers are often uncanny in their accuracy, right down to predicting dates and times when changes will be announced. Later you may even find yourself entertained to notice just how precise those rumors were.

Nonetheless, it's important to beware of the rumor mills! The hunches are not always correct and can cause great unnecessary anxiety. Unfortunately, the one thing those people spreading the rumors always seem to get wrong is the *reason* for the impending action. Usually, there is the tendency to assign blame to someone and this only confuses everyone involved. This then transforms an already difficult situation into one that is dangerously hateful, fueling the flames of anger throughout the organization.

As for non-work-related changes, here too, there is usually some sort of sign that change is in the offing.

Although we are often "warned" of an impending change, that is no consolation at all. Besides, the next stage is where we first recognize a significant emotional "bump."

In my position as a consultant, I always advise managers to make the announcement as soon as possible. There is tremendous pain for people in an organization where a change is imminent but delayed. This happens all too often. So much time goes by that it seems like everybody and his dog knows that something is about to happen and nerves start to fray. The atmosphere gets stranger and stranger. This is a miserable situation that could easily be avoided.

Shock

This is sure to hit just about everyone. Often, we don't really see that it has set in. It's others around us who tell us that we're acting strangely – that we don't seem like ourselves and we are not sticking with our normal routines.

Well, although we may have seen the change coming, perhaps with precision, we are still quite shocked when the announcement at work is actually made or when the CHANGE actually occurs.

I think that this occurs because we have left the world of "potential" and entered "reality". Now, fears confirmed, we are confronted in real-time with a new reality that is unfamiliar and extremely unsettling.

We had predicted this change. The problem is, at that moment we still feel like somebody has given us a punch in the gut. We may feel a little weak. Disoriented. Confused.

Denial

Here's the irony of the matter. We are invested in our current situation. We feel comfortable with the old and familiar, even if the situation is not ideal. Because the threat of change is accompanied by feelings of frustration and fear, we often choose to rationalize even obvious signs and pretend that things will remain the same.

You will see this phenomenon in others. By definition, none of us can see this in ourselves. It can seem absurd. *Someone who is in a state of denial is unable to see the obvious staring them right in the face.*

Often, those close to us will need to point out that we are making statements that are not logical, an imposition we find most unwelcome. You see, to us everything we are saying seems perfectly reasonable. We will be frustrated that everyone around us just doesn't get it and seems to be picking on us when we are down.

The most common statements of denial come in forms like these:

- "They'll reverse this decision."

- "Why, they can't possibly have thought this through."
- "I know that it's just a matter of time before they come to their senses."
- "They can't possibly get by without me (or Sam, or whomever)."
- "I'll just sit by the phone and wait. I'll give them 48 hours. They'll be calling and begging me to come back, and everything will be back to normal." And so on.

I would like to point out here that this is a typical reaction. Just about everybody shuts his or her eyes to the reality of the situation, at least for a little while. Those blinders give us the illusion of being safe. However, if we continue to deny the truth beyond a day or two, then we will begin to slide down a slippery slope where we put far too much energy into maintaining the denial. Hence, we won't have enough energy left to begin to heal and certainly not enough to begin to move forward.

Anger

Well, here's a familiar feeling for most of us, especially during a tumultuous transition. You didn't ask to be put into this situation, so you will naturally feel resentful. Don't let it alarm you. You're just like all of the rest of us.

When you are feeling dazed and confused by the chaos you once called your life, you will likely look for a culprit to blame for causing you all this misery. Ah, the Blame Game! I see this happen every single time an organization undergoes a major change. People are quite predictably unhappy with the change. And, invariably, there is a loud and sure voice that rises from the group to identify WHO is at fault (usually found circulating in The Gossip Mill, the hot topic at the water cooler). Yep, it happens every time. If it hasn't surfaced yet in your organization, just wait.

Although anger is ever so predictable, it is rare for anyone to act upon that anger in any overt way. I think the real danger is that the rage blinds people, making them unable to see what options are available. Rather than taking advantage of benefits, training, placement and career development that might be offered by management, the affected employee declines the help because he or she is just too "frosted" to accept anything from the perceived "enemy."

Fear

Notice what is happening. We are now moving from the old reality to a new reality. That means we are leaving the **KNOWN** and entering the **UNKNOWN**.

This is very scary for most of us. Even as painful as our old reality may have been, it was familiar. We knew, if nothing else, how to handle it in our way, how to survive. You know the old saying, "better to deal with the devil you know". The change brings with it uncharted territory. We don't know what is lurking around the bend, and we don't have a map to get to our desired destination.

I believe fear underlies all the other emotions on this "Waves of Change" chart. And fear is a powerful emotion that has the potential to paralyze us if we are not careful.

What do we all fear? We fear that we may NOT find a satisfactory resolution to our situation. We fear that we will let someone down, ourselves perhaps. We fear that the successes and the happy times we once enjoyed will never return. In short, we lose confidence and begin to doubt our ability and self-worth. This is to be expected, but it is painful, nonetheless.

Fear is an integral part of being human and it is absurd to pretend that it can easily be eliminated. In fact, we need fear to warn us of danger.

So when we are feeling fear, it is important to acknowledge and appreciate it. Treat fear like an old friend, a friend that has doubtlessly "saved" us from harm our entire lifetime. Once we've allowed ourselves to feel the fear, we can then release it.

Bargaining

We all do this when we are anxious. Bargaining is when we start making deals with ourselves, saying that maybe we don't have to change completely - maybe just a little.

A good example of this is the person who has been told that his or her job in the company has been eliminated and he or she must leave. Very often, after a little time has passed, that person comes back to the manager with a suggestion that they be given a part-time position. I once met a person in this circumstance who offered to work part-time for no pay. Of course, he was thinking that the company would reverse its decision and that by being there he would be put into a paid position.

In that circumstance, the man's wife was the one to clarify the situation for him, explaining that the entire family had gotten quite used to eating with some regularity. Would you believe that for a brief period he was resentful of her intrusion?

Well, that's bargaining. It's not a terrible thing really. The problem is, for the most part, it doesn't work. So, you don't want to waste too much precious time pretending.

Acceptance

Yes, eventually acceptance occurs for everybody. This is the moment when we can clearly recognize that the Change is here to stay. There is no longer room for doubt or denial. We have stopped going in circles, and an important thing has returned to our lives – certainty. We are now sure about the turn of events, for better or worse.

Ideally, rather than just resigning ourselves to our predicament, we now realize this twist of fate provides an opportunity to embark on a new, fascinating journey.

Hope

Well, of course, this is the point where, having accepted that something has indeed changed, we have an *expectation* that we will eventually reach our new destination. This is what most of us consider to be a welcome occurrence. We realize the Change we face provides us with an opportunity to reflect on past achievements, to take stock of our lives, to pursue unrealized dreams, and, perhaps, to explore our true calling.

Here's another common occurrence.

Depression

I tell all of my clients that depression is not unusual during a time of change. The "blue" feelings should pass quickly. But if the sadness *does* continue beyond a few weeks, consider consulting your physician.

How can I tell if I am depressed?

A couple of the most common experiences that my clients have reported over the years have been with two fundamental functions of life: Eating and Sleeping! When either of these two goes awry, our ability to perform at top notch can be impaired. So it is worth our while to **pay attention** so that we can maintain the energy we need to make a smooth and triumphant transition.

If you notice that you have suddenly become ravenous, ready to eat anything in sight, or you have gone to other extremes where eating seems like a terrible burden, try to remember that, without a healthy body it will be difficult to achieve any goal you have set for yourself. If you cannot seem to get your eating habits in control, seek help.

The same holds true for sleeping. In the sleep arena, think also in terms of habits. We all have a natural rhythm, an internal clock that is set just for us. What is your "normal pattern"? What is the time you get up naturally, without an alarm clock? If we stay in rhythm with our preprogrammed schedule, we function at our best and feel in-sync.

Here's another food for thought:

Three Ways of "Leaving"

I feel this is an appropriate time to share an observation that I have made repeatedly over the years.

At the point when we *leave* behind something in life, be it a job, a relationship, a home, or any other significant aspect of our lives, we separate in three ways: *emotionally, psychologically and physically.*

I'm sure you've witnessed the same thing.

Let's look at the way a person leaves a job or a relationship, for example.

First:
Emotionally Leaving – This is the point at which a person stops caring whether the job gets done or the relationship is enjoyable. In some cases, individuals may continue to be concerned about the quality of work being performed or the whereabouts and activities of the estranged former partner, for weeks, months, or even years after the job or relationship has ended.

> Conversely, when a person decides to leave a relationship or job for another opportunity, it is not unusual to stop caring long before he or she leaves.

> By the way, as for the job situation, our attitude of caring is quite visible to our colleagues and bosses. This is often the way that others predict that we are about to make a change before we tell them. And certainly, this is so often true in a relationship where the partner notices things avoided and unstated and draws conclusions – often, accurately.

Second:
Psychologically Leaving– In a job loss situation, this entails the degree to which someone is *thinking* about details of their job, irrespective of whether the individual is still physically performing their duties.

In relationship break-ups, one or both partners often obsess about the details of life together long after the end – such as wondering about the other's activities, what are third parties thinking about the partners, and the like.

For example, during job lay-offs, I have seen people be asked to physically leave the building immediately, yet they continue to think about the work despite their removal. They call their former boss or their colleagues on several occasions to check on details even though they are no longer present to manage the work. This can go on for several weeks, but eventually the calls cease as the person's attention is turned to their job search, or a new job.

The point is, we have a clear need to be involved psychologically. We seek it. We naturally feel a painful void when we no longer have an intellectual outlet in our lives.

By the way, this is a significant but under examined issue for new retirees. But that is a topic for later in this book.

And Third:
Physically Leaving – Yes, at some point we *physically* leave a job or a relationship.

I advocate a "clean break" whenever possible. By this I mean that, if you have a choice, leave quickly, not over time. The sooner that we are physically relocated, the sooner the other two phases of leaving can "catch up."

We need the energy that all three of these aspects require in order to do our best in our job search, our next job, and/or our transition to the next relationship.

Self-Management

Being aware of which one of the stages we are experiencing helps us manage the transition with greater finesse. It is also useful to recognize, if we can, the stages our associates are undergoing at any given time when they are facing the same major change we are at the workplace. This allows you to avoid taking things personally or avoid jumping to conclusions that have the potential to cause greater conflict and undue stress. There is no sense in compounding the already tense situation, if you can avoid it.

Above all, recognize that these stages are temporary. Eventually, EVERYBODY arrives at a new phase, a phase they find more comfortable. There is no reason to believe that you will be any different. In fact, more than likely, you have been through similar circumstances before and have ultimately triumphed over the adversity. It is easy to forget this fact when during a new, unfolding Change episode. Try to recall these past victories when you begin to feel anxious this time around.

Prepare for Awkwardness and Ambiguity

There seems to be no experience of Change that occurs without a fair amount of awkwardness and ambiguity. We feel unsure, as though we are "lost in the dark."

This is new, this specific situation. There's no script to follow. They don't teach a course in "Dealing with Change" in school. And there are so few, if any, "role models" for change.

Even our numerous experiences in the past with the inevitable changes that occur in life, don't seem to help us feel adequately "prepared".

And, because we feel apprehensive and insecure, the people around us– our family, our friends, and our coworkers– are not usually sure how to relate to us. That's one of those ironies. We don't know quite how to act for a while, and the people around us don't know how to act, either. Now THAT is awkward.

Awareness is the first step in being able to turn things around. Once we understand the dynamics, we can manage them. In other words, if you know things are going to feel awkward, you won't be caught off guard so you won't feel the same emotional punch. Awareness allows you to get some distance from the situation, a perspective that will enable you to just observe and then make sound decisions.

Patience and Curiosity

And, finally, patience and curiosity are the two tools I have found to be invaluable and strongly recommend become an integral part of your change management plan are patience and curiosity.

The worst thing to do at the beginning of a Change event in our lives is to act in haste, making rash decisions and bold statements before assessing the situation thoroughly. Herein lies a dangerous trap, one that leads many people to allow their emotions to dictate critical choices.

But as with all other times of our lives, *choices have consequences.* If I can spare you in some major area, this may be the one

You see, in the many years that I have worked with people who are experiencing a radical Change, the most common misstep is to do or say something before enough of the facts have been evaluated to make a reasoned choice.

For example: When told that their job has been eliminated and that they will leave the employer after a transitional period, too many people have chosen to express their anger by shutting down their performance. This, from the outside looking in, may seem quite reasonable. After all, the company has said that they no longer need you, so why care about how well you perform in the last days and hours? But by choosing to be lackadaisical, you may be shooting yourself in the foot. It is possible that even though one job has been eliminated, other jobs may become available prior to your departure. How ironic!

Yet, I have often been privy to this very scenario. The departing employee, after several weeks of noticeably declining performance in response to being "laid off," applies for a position that constitutes a promotion. But oops, the opportunity may be lost for no good reason because management will have to take into consideration their observations from the most recent period.

Well, how can we manage the very natural anger that arises? The most effective strategy that I have seen (and personally applied) is to arouse your *CURIOSITY!*

By this I mean to ask questions – lots of questions. What really is happening here? You will find, as I have, that this is the ideal remedy for operating with too little information. Also, when we are in the process of asking for clarification, our anger in a situation very naturally subsides.

It's quite simple and uncanny.

A Story – Inquisitiveness Gives Us an Edge

I was once approached for coaching by an employee who was having a severe problem with a co-worker. Because the organization was closing its office in a few months, the level of anxiety in the workplace was enormous.

The employee who approached me, I'll call her "Shirley," explained that her co-worker "Laura", was not trying to get the work done, and this was affecting Shirley's ability to do her job.

Shirley explained that her conversations with Laura had not persuaded Laura to try any harder. But Shirley admitted that her statements to Laura had been accusatory, and Laura had reacted defensively.

I suggested that Shirley talk with Laura again but stick to asking questions *only*. What was Laura feeling? Why was she feeling this way? What could Laura do to pick up production? How could Shirley support her more effectively? And so forth.

Shirley called me a few days later to say that Laura had responded *very* positively this time and that they had agreed to work together to be successful until the very day that the office closed.

Shirley remarked that Laura had really changed and that it was remarkable.

I reminded Shirley that it was *she* who had changed, by her approach. She was asking questions that sounded *supportive* rather than making statements that sounded accusatory and judgmental.

It seems to me we all deserve to give each other some slack in an emotionally charged time of change. Remember, the style with which we communicate to one another sends a message of either helpful camaraderie or divisiveness.

Also, I have used the questioning style to diffuse my own anger in a situation. I find that, as I formulate questions I can divert my energy, away from my irrational anger and towards satisfying my curiosity about the "what" and the "why."

Have you noticed how easy it is to experience anger over an event (almost immediately upon the first reports of a situation), only to learn later that the initial facts were inaccurate?

If you can remind yourself about the danger of making assumptions, you will be doing yourself a tremendous favor. If you find the process difficult, try this: When someone does or says something that seems totally irrational and pushes some button that causes your blood to start boiling, just respond by saying, "hmm." Continue to do this until you feel your anger diffuses enough that you can start asking questions.

This process of "switching" from anger to curiosity allows us to manage the feelings in our lives in a far more reasonable and productive manner.

Remember: There is always a "Back Story".

While on this point, I would like to share an additional and related concept.

Have you ever noticed, in yourself or in others, that it is so easy to become angry at the behavior of others, and it seems to always arise in a "flash"?

Let's say you are driving along in congested traffic and someone changes lanes in front of you without any signal. Our immediate assessment is often, "He/she cut me off!". At this kind of moment, many of us begin to fantasize about pulling that driver out of their car and thumping them thoroughly. This is a common reaction, so we are not unusual if this is our first reaction.

At such a moment as this, pay attention to what you are feeling inside. Your anger has given rise to your blood pressure. Your heart is, usually, pounding like crazy. Your body temperature feels like it has risen dramatically (it probably has). You find yourself imagining all manner of effrontery that this other driver has visited upon us. We assume that the driver's carelessness was intentional and aimed specifically at us.

Oh, isn't all of this so common?

Here's a way to unpack this situation.

First, we really have no idea about what is really going on or motivating the other driver. Right?

It is all together possible that the other driver has had a death in the family and is rushing home to be with grieving family.

The other driver may have just been told that his job has been eliminated and he was marched off his company's premises without any notice. So, this has made that driver, at the same time, frightened for the future, angry at the callous way the job termination was conducted. And, so forth.

The point is, we have witnessed someone's apparent reckless behavior without knowing the circumstances that have led up to that moment for the careless driving. All of this may have a cause that, if we knew, or were in their shoes, we could understand and immediately forgive the seeming effrontery.

A story

There is a story that I have heard several times recently that helps to illustrate this concept.

It seems that a man was nervously pacing back and forth in a hospital Waiting Room. His young daughter had fallen from her bicycle and fractured her arm and she was in considerable pain. The nurses told the father that they had paged the duty orthopedic surgeon to come into the hospital to operate on the daughter's arm and reset it and they were just keeping his daughter as comfortable as possible while they waited.

As time passed, the father became more and more enraged by the amount of time that it was taking for the surgeon to arrive and get started. He kept asking the nurses and they assured him that the doctor had acknowledged his page and promised to come to the hospital as soon as he could possibly get there.

But the father was sure that the surgeon was just taking his sweet time to come in – probably finishing his golf game, or something similar.

After a couple of hours, the surgeon arrived and came into the Waiting Room to explain the operative plan and to get the father's consent.

The father exploded at the doctor. He berated the surgeon for not caring about the daughter's pain and discomfort and promising to register a complaint to the hospital's board and try to get the doctor fired.

The surgeon apologized as best he could, got the father's signature permission for the operation, and returned to the Operating Room to scrub for the procedure.

After the operation was successfully completed, the doctor came to advise the father of the perfect outcome, only to be yelled at and berated, and threatened, yet again.

The surgeon left the Waiting Room and then the hospital without a word to anyone.

Later, when the father was sitting with his now comfortable daughter in her Recovery Room, a nurse entered to change her dressing. The father seized the opportunity to share his anger with the nurse about the surgeon's tardiness and his intention to report him for his behavior.

The nurse turned to the father and told him that she knew that the surgeon was in fact unavailable, but the closest qualified surgeon for the operation that the daughter required.

Then the nurse shared that the surgeon was late because he had been attending the funeral of his own young daughter who had died from a fall and broken neck. The surgeon had been unable to save his own daughter.

Nonetheless, the doctor had agreed to leave the funeral and gravesite and rush to the hospital with all speed.

The angry father looked at his own daughter, now healing and sure to recover completely. She had been helped by another father who had just lost his own daughter, but braced through his own intense sadness in order to help another father's daughter.

The angry father did not lodge his threatened complaint.

The moral of this story is quite clear.

In fact, when any of us gets angry, assuming a slight from another person, the truth is that we just never know the backstory. What has happened in this situation that I do not see and cannot know?

But, always, there IS a backstory. There are reasons that cause others to act in apparently inappropriate ways. Yet, as we judge the behavior of another, basing our judgement entirely on what we have seen – the surface- all the while there is usually another story that has preceded the person's actions that may well form an entirely different reality to what we have witnessed.

Where do emotions come from? Externally? Or Internally?

And this brings us to the deeper glaring reality of such an emotionally charged reaction. You see, I am certain that "anger" is a condition of one's life that lies dormant inside of us. When the perfect external stimulus occurs, the anger that is alive inside of us comes to the surface.

That's it. I don't believe that most emotions exist outside of ourselves and have been visited upon us, causing us to feel a way.

So, the fact is that when a situation happens and we exhibit anger (or love, or hurt feelings, etc.), it is because the external occurrence has given our inner life the opportunity to display the otherwise dormant emotion.

So, this is a critical distinction and necessary to master, if we are ever to find joy and contentment.

We only act-out an emotion, such as anger, which was already inside of us. The life-improving challenge, then, is to recognize this and work to identify the source of the emotion's existence within, and determine to manage that emotion from within. Once we learn this skill, we will be happier in our day-to-day living and enjoy all occurrences in our environment.

Clear Sailing over the Horizon

Remember that, regardless of what you are feeling at this point in your current Change experience, you *will* get through this. Not only will you get through this, you really will be okay on the other side. Ultimately, we are all resilient beings with a deep reservoir of inner strength.

It's important to never lose sight of the true "treasures" in our lives as we continue on our journey of Change. Your loved ones will stick by you during this new voyage of discovery, and the beauty that surrounds you will continue to shine as you explore new horizons. Even if you encounter tumultuous waves that rock the boat, clear skies will return. When you reach your destination, you will be richer and wiser for the experience and more prepared for the next Change voyage.

CHAPTER 3

Managing Change: Strategies for Success

Every Single Day, in Even the Simplest Way:
- ☐ Care for our Mind (Seek to Learn)
- ☐ Care for our Body (Master Moderation)
- ☐ Care for our Spirit (Practice Appreciation)

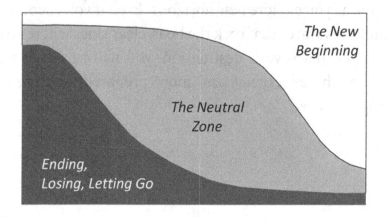

WHEN EACH OF us makes the <u>decision</u> to change something in our lives, that is one thing. But often, as may be the case for you right now, some force outside of us may have made a decision that has turned our lives upside down.

We may have no control over this Change that has been made for us. We may have lost a job due to a company policy to let people go. We might have lost a mate due to an accident or even his or her decision to terminate the relationship.

It is at times like these that it is so important that we treat ourselves with care, making sure we develop a successful plan for nurturing our entire being that includes: expanding our mind, caring for our body, and enriching our spirit. These measures are essential to maintain health and strength, crucial qualities needed to chart a new course through the turbulent waves of unwanted and unexpected change.

During times of radical Change, when it seems as though our lives are lost at sea, the best way to get back on course is to focus on ways to treat ourselves with tender loving care. This may not guarantee that our jobs will be restored after a layoff or that we will meet the most perfect mate after a divorce or that we will be able to quickly shrug off the unfathomable grief after the death of a loved one. But it will ensure that we are in the best shape possible to deal effectively with any obstacles we may encounter.

Viktor Frankl, a Jewish psychiatrist, survived his internment in a concentration camp during the Holocaust by helping his fellow prisoners cope with their inhuman and unspeakable circumstances. He wrote of his experiences in a wonderful book, *Man's Search for Meaning.*

Frankl's observation is that it is not so important **what** happens to any of us during our lives. Rather, it matters only *__how__* *__we__* *__respond__* to these circumstances. Since many things that occur in our lives are beyond our control, why not concentrate on those things we *can* influence?

As we take charge of those things that are in the realm of our control, we are much more likely to ensure the desired result if we make a concerted effort every day to find balance and live in harmony– treating our mind, body and spirit as an integrated whole. Keep in mind these are the most precious tools we possess to **Live Well During Times of Change**.

If we become so preoccupied with the chaos on the outside and neglect the inside, it's easy to lose our way as the storm swirls around us. By honoring our mind, our body, and our spirit, even if it seems like a roundabout way to reach our destination, we can navigate with great skill and even enjoy the adventurous ride.

Strategy 1

Mind

There is a great deal of evidence to show that the mind must be maintained, just like any other part of the body. Have you seen the studies on aging that concluded people who remain intellectually stimulated have a dramatically higher likelihood of living longer and avoiding the ravages of Alzheimer's?

And, I'm sure you have noticed that during extremely stressful times it can become difficult to think clearly, and that high anxiety is often accompanied by lapses in judgment. In short, our mental faculties can come under direct assault during times of Change if we are not careful to cultivate our minds.

The mind is like any muscle. With exercise, it develops, growing sharper and keener. Without regular workouts, atrophy sets in. I have concluded that, during times of radical change it is essential we make sure to keep our mind in mint condition by stimulating our minds– by doing anything, from crossword puzzles to taking school courses.

Care for the Mind

Mind- (ME, fr. OE *gemynd):* **a**: the element or complex of elements in an individual that feels, perceives, thinks, wills, and especially reasons **b**: the conscious mental events and capabilities in an organism **c**: the organized conscious and unconscious adaptive mental activity of an organism

Miriam-Webster New Collegiate Dictionary

Ways to Expand Our Mind

☐ Sign Up for a Course
☐ Read Daily
☐ Keep a Journal
☐ Find a Mentor
☐ Adopt A Pervasive Sense of Humor

We are intellectual beings. We process information, we analyze, and we comprehend.

In the years that I have been counseling clients during times of radical change, I have observed tremendous benefits in the lives of those who have paid extra attention to increasing the capacity of their mind.

Caring for our minds, working at achieving excellent mental health and a positive mental attitude, as well as increasing mental acuity is just as important as caring for our physical well-being during times of Change.

Have you noticed that during extremely stressful times you may have trouble in thinking clearly? Your ability to make judgments that advance your own best interests may seem to slip in the face of high anxiety.

When one is experiencing Change such as being between jobs, it is important to keep mentally active. Boredom and lethargy can set in and can be just as detrimental as poor diet and no exercise.

Keep mentally active. Progress a little every day.

Some specific things to **DO:**

- Sign up for a course on some subject about which you have always been curious or that relates to new developments in your career field.
- Begin reading a new book, and stick to a daily reading schedule, even though your traumatized self will tell you there just isn't enough time.

- Start a journal. Set aside time each day to enter an account of what is happening in your life, as though you were sharing it with a loving parent who wants to know every detail.
- Find a mentor.
- Make room for a lot of humor. Go to a comedy club or just buy a joke book by your favorite cartoonist. You can never have too much laughter in your life. Remember, genuine belly laughs free the mind and release endorphins that help reduce stress.

These are only a few of the many things that my clients have done to exercise their minds.

What will *you* do?

Whatever you choose, Enjoy!

Learn Now - Learn Forever

This section is about lifelong learning and about the need to learn something new every single day. This becomes part of the daily "ritual" I recommend.

I think that the mind is like any muscle. With exercise, it develops and excels. Without regular workouts, atrophy sets in.

My teenage son just hates it when I talk about this lifelong need. But it has become clear to me that not a single one of us can ever stop learning.

This world in which we live is now far more than a "service economy." We have entered the "information age," which is now accompanied by the "information highway" on the Internet. And every day more and more sophisticated technology is being created to move and use information. All of this is happening at breakneck speed.

Why, by the time you go to the computer store to buy the latest version of a software program that you *just* saw advertised, the next version has already been shipped from the manufacturer, a fact that gives the clerk at the store great cause for amusement, knowing you'll be back again soon. They are putting this stuff out faster than we can keep up. But, keep up we must or we lose our competitive edge.

I ask employee groups the following question: How many jobs in this world do *not* require the use of technology? They are never able to cite very many.

I have been around this orb for a little over a half-century and have witnessed an impressive amount of changes in that time. For example, I worked as a checker at a grocery store while I was in college. This was a pretty good job in those days. Well, it paid union-level wages and it seemed easy, so I felt like I was taking an intellectual break from my studies while making the money I needed to pay the bills.

It wasn't too demanding. I had to distinguish one type of fruit from another, which items were on sale (they'd have the non-sale price stamped on them), and how to correctly pack a grocery bag. Oh, and excellent arithmetic skills were essential. This was needed to make correct change when we upgraded to cash registers. But first I remember adding the bill on the outside of the brown grocery bag.

I was thinking about those times the other evening as I waited in line at the local mega-grocery store. I watched as the clerk swiped all the items across a laser that read the bar codes and then did all the calculations. I thought at first that this person's job was ever so much simpler than mine so many years ago. But then there was a glitch. The machine seemed to freeze. Suddenly all the clerks were making hand signals to the manager's office or picking up their intercoms. The central computer for the store had temporarily stopped working. One of the managers was frantically taking instructions by phone and typing onto a keyboard at the front. We waited helplessly for several minutes. Then the manager announced over the intercom that the problem was resolved but each clerk would have to "re-boot" his or her station. I watched the clerk type words and numbers into her console with ease, and very quickly her machine began to work again. Everything was back to normal. The process continued.

Well, this really caused me to reconsider my assumption that her job was so much easier than the one I had so many years ago. After all, I had just watched her enter data with great facility. What skill set does this kind of ability require? Not one that even existed when I was a grocery checkout clerk.

So, if most jobs require the use of technology and technologies change so constantly, what must each of us do to keep up? *We just must keep learning - our entire lives.* It is a huge mistake to believe that we have "arrived" and possess all that we need to know. It's most useful, I think, to just *get* that **we can never stop learning.**

Read Daily

The acquisition of new knowledge requires time and effort. Certainly, we learn from conversations with colleagues, instructional videos, or by attending a lecture. But there is no substitute for reading to gain depth and breadth of knowledge necessary to be a success.

It may be that reading is not your strong suit. But we need to read to excel. The challenge is to find the motivation and the time to read: TO LEARN.

The best strategy for those of us who are reading-challenged is to set a daily schedule for reading. The amount of time set aside can be as little as 15 to 30 minutes a day. The key to progress is consistency. Now, admittedly, our "little voices" are likely to speak up and tell us that we just can't spare that much time each day. After all, we must deal with the ramifications of the momentous change that has recently wreaked havoc in our lives. Well, if this is your feeling, you're surely not alone.

Many times, during my workshops, I have heard "push back" from participants, claiming time scarcity as a reason for not adopting a daily reading regimen. Since ninety percent of the attendees at my workshops have come because they are between jobs, you would think that they have plenty of spare time. But the truth is, because they are facing the trauma of change, they are feeling psychologically and emotionally wounded, a state that makes it difficult to follow even the best of advice.

In fact, we usually can find the time we need when we are clearheaded and purposeful. The "I don't have the time" excuse is just that, an excuse, something we delude ourselves into believing when we are in pain. A boss of mine used to say; "There's *always* a reason not to do things...."

So, what I suggest is, see the excuse for what it is, an obstacle standing in the way of our progress. Acknowledge that fact, and determine to move forward, even if only by "baby steps." Five minutes a day can seem so difficult at first, but in no time the five minutes will fly by, and then you can move on to ten, then fifteen, then twenty.

You probably already know that this kind of incremental progress works with any task in life that challenges us. "A thousand miles starts with the first step."

Keep a Journal

One of the most rewarding things I have done for my personal growth is to start a journal.

Every day during stressful times I spend some time writing about the day's events. I force myself to express how the events of the day made me *feel*. I say force, because initially I found it a bit uncomfortable to express my feelings, even on paper. Perhaps I found it difficult because, as a guy, emotional disclosure was never something I was encouraged to develop growing up. But despite my reticence at the beginning, journaling has proved to be invaluable on my journey of discovery.

Writing has helped me bring my thoughts into clear focus as I reflect on the day and the impact various events had on me. In this way, I can get a handle on my anger, fear, and similar emotions that are too risky to share with just anyone.

If I am angry with someone, I practice "telling" him or her about my feelings until I have calmed down. This can be such a valuable exercise since I know that people put up their defenses very quickly when they feel that they are being attacked. Journaling has allowed me to release the full brunt of my anger so that by the time I speak with the person, I can be calm and rational.

I heartily recommend keeping a journal to manage emotions and gain greater insight into our hearts and souls.

Find a Mentor

The idea that we can do things on our own is about as American as it gets. Rugged individualism is a revered quality in this country. The problem is that as individuals we lack objectivity and perspective when we are too close to our problems. Sharing our struggles with someone who has gone through a similar transition provides us with a fresh point of view and greater understanding of the situation.

The problem is that many of us are reluctant to reveal our struggles because we are afraid we will be exposing our weaknesses and vulnerabilities. As much as I try to avoid gross generalizations, I find this reticence is most often found in men. Given the kinds of training that most men were given as they grew up, this is understandable.

An extreme example of this type of behavior was described in a newspaper article *by New York Times* Tokyo bureau chief Howard French. In the article entitled "The Pretenders," Mr. French described how, in Japan, for some people, namely middle-aged men, "losing a job is so shameful that they will do anything to keep the world from finding out."

Mr. French gave the stark example of one Japanese worker, an appraiser, who began a life of make-believe and disguise after he lost his job. He shared that no one in his family had told anyone that he had been let go. But even more debilitating was his inability to face the world. He had only been able to go to the government unemployment agency once; bumping into an acquaintance would be too hard to explain. Even traveling seemed out of the realm of possibility because he was afraid his neighbors would grow suspicious. Instead, he settled into a fixed routine, as regular and confining as the life of a prisoner.

If you recognize yourself in any part of this story, please do your best to find the strength to overcome your objections. At least try it for just a little while. We are social beings and fare far better when we reach out for support rather than trying to go it alone.

I have found it to be enormously valuable to find even a single individual whom I can trust to act as a sounding board and "coach" to help me navigate through tough times. Ideally, I try to choose someone who has experienced a comparable situation to the one in which I find myself.

If nothing else, this valued guide, or mentor, has a sense of objectivity. Although he or she may have experienced similar circumstances at some point, this person is not emotionally or physically involved, so the mentor is able to give me sound advice about my circumstances and can help me think things through in a calm, rational manner–*before* I respond.

I would compare this type of guide, my mentor, to a ringside manager in the world of boxing where the fighter relies heavily on his advice between rounds. Since the boxer is completely focused on his opponent in each round and must cope with the pain of constant combat, he is far from objective in assessing his performance and technique.

However, because the manager is outside the ring, he can observe every nuance that is taking place in the ring. This gives him the ability to provide objective advice, free of any pain or fear the fighter might be feeling.

And, of course, just as in life, the coach never jumps into the ring to relieve the contestant for a couple of rounds. No one, not even the most valued counsel, is ever going to take over our problems for us. Naturally, when we are under intense pressure, finding someone to stand in for us would seem like the perfect answer to our predicament. As enticing as that scenario might seem, it's not reality.

Besides, anyone else "working" a problem in our stead robs us of the true benefit of improving ourselves which only happens from facing problems and working them out – for ourselves – but with competent coaching.

What is certain is that having a coach who can guide us from "outside the ring" during confusing and chaotic change events in our lives will prove to be an invaluable asset.

Humor

Take some time–every single day– to find a way to laugh. No matter how difficult our situation may seem, we are always capable of laughter. Maybe we are hard-pressed to find humor in our situation now, but if we make a conscious effort, we can always find something to smile about. If we find a way to suspend our seriousness and negativity, if even for a brief time, we will reap dividends in our physical health and mental well-being.

So. Go ahead. Laugh. It won't hurt. And it may just shift your life in a positive direction. And this is, after all, where it belongs.

Strategy 2

Care for the Body

- ☐ Healthy Living Every Day in Some Small Way
- ☐ Exercise and Nutrition
- ☐ Sleep Strategies
- ☐ Stick with Routine
- ☐ Laughter– the Elixir
- ☐ Teach yourself to separate the trivial from the profound.

The pursuit of a healthy body–health, strength, and attractiveness–is not narcissistic. On the contrary, attention to proper exercise, nutrition, and sleep, especially when one has experienced a significant life Change is essential for maintaining a successful self-image and deep self-confidence.

Healthy Living Every Day in Some Small Way

I'd like to share some tips I learned from observing many people who have dealt with radical Change by doing something, be it ever so small, *every day* for their bodies. It has helped them to survive the stressful times. And more importantly, it has contributed greatly to their ability to Live Well During Times of Change.

If you strive to achieve balance in your life, you will find the resulting harmony that helps you stay focused and calm. This state of being contributes to a positive attitude, which in turn has a profound effect on our health and general well-being.

Exercise and Nutrition

Well, here I go into very touchy territory for most people. But my purpose here is not to serve as a weight-loss coach or exercise guru. I simply want to remind you gently that your body will only perform as well as you treat it. Since our bodies are inexorably intertwined with our minds, to function optimally, *it is essential to pay attention to every aspect of our health.*

Here, **moderation is the key**.

My grandfather was a classic country doctor. He used to tell me that, when it comes to things physical, moderation and consistency are the keys to living a long life.

I raise this point because I have observed that many men and women with whom I have worked who were undergoing a radical Change reported that they also and simultaneously became worried about their appearance, suddenly self-conscious that their weight would create a negative impression when interviewing for a new job.

To respond to this anxiety, some set out on an intense exercise and diet program. The problem with this approach, given all the other stressors that accompany a momentous change, is that the added pressure of trying to fit back into an old college outfit is often a recipe for failure.

And failure is the last thing anyone needs when facing the upheaval that accompanies a major life change. I believe a far better way to spend the time and energy you would have put toward dieting is to make a concerted effort to appreciate yourself just the way you are. This positive attitude translates into better general health and a self-image that projects confidence and poise. It is an undeniable fact that our outlook on life influences our bodies in countless ways.

It is also critical to acknowledge that physical flexibility and a sense of balance are essential to enjoy life to the fullest. To achieve these qualities, a moderate routine of regular exercise is essential. We all have heard the saying, "use it or lose it." When it comes to muscles, if they are left idle, they will atrophy. This is often what happens to older folks who lose their equilibrium and flexibility as they age. But this phenomenon does not happen overnight. This deterioration takes place over time as major muscle groups are neglected.

To avoid this problem, establish a moderate exercise routine and stick to it every day. Just a handful of stretches and light exercise will keep the muscles strengthened and toned, enabling us to utilize our bodies to their fullest capacity.

So, it's worth repeating: Moderation is the key to maintaining a healthy body.

Eat sensibly and exercise a bit every day.

Don't be surprised if, after a while you find yourself wanting to work out even more because it feels so good.

Just as our lives can change, so can our bodies. Although we can't turn back the hands of time, we can easily increase the amount we move, which will greatly improve our agility and general state of well-being.

Sleep Strategies

When life takes an unexpected turn, it is not unusual to experience a variety of emotional cycles: highs and lows, slight depression, anxiety.

Sleep is often affected during times of unwanted change. Either tossing and turning becomes a nightly ritual or the bedcover suddenly feels as though it has been stuffed with lead, and it seems impossible to get out of bed.

Don't worry. Almost everybody experiences changes in their sleep patterns when experiencing pressure and stress.

Without a doubt, this stage is sure to pass, and you will be able to return to your normal rhythm.

We all have our typical sleeping patterns. Most of us need 6 to 9 hours of sleep per night. I am one who needs 5 to 6 to function, but I feel the best if I have gotten 7 hours of sleep the night before. On the other hand, I do not feel that I am at my best if I sleep for more than 8 hours. Now that's a change for me from my younger years when I used to enjoy the rare opportunity to saw logs for 10 hours or so on a Saturday night. The point here is: try to tune into your inner clock so that you can perform at your peak.

Stick with Routine

In general, during periods when we feel as though our lives have been turned upside down, we can take a great deal of comfort from our general routines. Here I mean the little things. Try to stick to your familiar schedule, the times that you are used to doing the mundane things like eating and sleeping. We associate these routines with comfort and normalcy. They remind us that we are okay and that life really does go on, no matter how painful the current change may feel.

The times of the day when we eat, watch TV, shower, fetch the mail or do homework with the kids– these are all routines that are familiar to us. They serve as a framework for our lives, providing familiarity and security.

If the change that you are experiencing right now is the loss of your job, it is important to stick with your norms between the time you left your previous employment and when you start your new job. You may not like this idea. It seems like such an enticing idea to crawl under the covers and catch up on a decade of lost sleep. But my clients have told me that they have been very grateful for the following suggestions, even though they didn't believe that they would make a difference before they tried them.

Suggestion # l: Even though you may not have any appointments on your schedule or any pressing tasks on any given day, *get up!*

Yes, I mean you, and you know who you are. Get yourself up. Set your alarm and stay on the same schedule you followed when you were actively employed.

You will find that, unless you stick with your natural schedule, you will not feel quite "right" all day.

Haven't you noticed that before?

Each of us has an internal clock, one that is set for our optimal performance. If we tune in to our subconscious and synchronize with our natural rhythm, we will function at our best.

So, if you have been used to getting up at 6 a.m. every morning for the last twenty years your inner clock is set for that time. Furthermore, the time you normally rise becomes a part of your self-image, one that you associate with success. If you alter the time that you wake up, you risk the possibility of lowering your self-esteem, the last thing you need when you are in the throes of change, the process of a job search or getting adjusted to any new life circumstance.

So, even if it's a little difficult to muster your will power, please try to follow this suggestion in spite of your very natural resistance. In the long run, you will be glad that you did. You will be in the company of a large number of people who found this advice to be very helpful, even if they only came to this conclusion in retrospect.

Suggestion # 2: Now, if you didn't like Suggestion # 1, you're just going to *hate* this one. But here it is. While you are at home during your time of transition, even on days that you do not have any specific plans, *get dressed*. That's correct. You read it accurately. I mean put on presentable clothes, the kind you would wear when you go out for the world to see.

You ask, why bother? Because the way we dress sends a message. That's a truism in our culture. So, if you stay in your pj's, you are telling yourself, at least subconsciously, that nothing you do throughout the day is important. If you string enough days like that together, it is easy to start feeling that nothing matters, that the efforts you are making are pointless, an attitude that can pull you down a dangerous spiral.

Laughter– the Elixir

I have read with great interest the work of Dr. Norman Vincent Peale. You may remember his books, *The Power of Positive Thinking,* or *The Power of Positive Living.* He asserted that people who live positive, upbeat lives are the healthiest people and can make miraculous recoveries from illness and other difficulties. Another well-known author and former editor of the *Saturday Review of Literature,* Norman Cousins, in his book, *Anatomy of Illness* suggested laughter and humor as a cure for sickness.

At the suggestion of a most trusted mentor, I have made a conscious decision to laugh and smile every day of my life. It has become my hallmark. People now say that they feel comfortable around me. They say that I lift their spirits. People respond more positively to an optimistic person, they find it reassuring and inspiring.

The health benefits are undeniable. Although I have spent most of my adult life no less than 75 pounds overweight, I rarely get sick. But I have come to say, I *never* get sick, because that is the way I feel.

Even though I have developed an irritating ailment that debilitates many fellow sufferers, I refuse to see it as "chronic," I have never felt inclined to research it nor am I ever able to remember any details about the disease. This is because I decline to acknowledge its permanence. Instead, I see it as a temporary condition. In fact, I use some of my more amusing hospital tales to entertain my friends and myself. Indeed, if you choose to be open to it, you can find humor in almost every situation.

Let me remind you of my determination to live to be one hundred years of age. I do not consider this just a frivolous statement; *rather it is my conscious choice.* I have already passed the halfway mark but I still have too much to accomplish before I call it quits this time around. I am convinced that my cheerfulness and constant efforts to remain positive and wear a smile will assure my longevity. I plan to laugh my way to the century mark.

I think that some of the people I have met depend on their illness to fill a void of affection. They mistakenly interpret sympathy as fondness. A far more effective strategy to make faithful friends is to become someone who is a joy to be around.

Suggestion # 1: Find a friend with whom you can share a joke or light story every day. Don't let a day go by without a laugh. Laughing is potent medicine for the soul.

Suggestion # 2: To gain perspective, contemplate the relative importance of events in your life. Learn to distinguish the trivial from the profound.

Attending to and caring for our body is not just about weight management. Making sure we incorporate a daily routine of exercise, attention to nutrition, and eating in moderation is always sound advice, but even more essential when we feel life has pulled the rug out from under our feet.

Every single day, do something for your body. It is not so important what, just do. Every positive action will always render a positive effect.

Strategy 3

Spirit

The spirit is a little more elusive and difficult to define. Many people think that when I begin discussing this topic in one of my workshops, I am certainly about to talk about religion, but this is not so.

Remember the story of the hidden jewel in Chapter 1. Spirit is that hidden jewel in our lives that holds the promise of living a rich and rewarding life. Our spirit includes *what we believe* because our convictions provide the means to uncover our buried treasure within

People need to believe in something to take any action whatsoever, be it using the ATM machine or helping a friend. But for most of us, our beliefs are deeply buried in our subconscious. We generally pay little attention to what it is that we believe, so we often end up functioning on autopilot. We just do things and make up "stories" later to try to explain why we did what we did. Psychologists call this rationalization. I call it human.

But an unexamined life is not a terribly helpful way to live. It's important to make a conscious effort to reflect on our beliefs and behavior to ensure we are living an authentic and purposeful life. Only when we take some time to examine whether our actions and words match our fundamental values and passion for life, can we ensure that we are following our inner compass toward our personal dreams and aspirations. Sometimes we need to embark on a journey of inner exploration before we can determine where it is we want to go.

Only when we seek the truth and attempt to identify our deeply-held beliefs can we discover any attitudes we hold that work against us. Once we recognize our misguided views, we can replace them with more positive and productive ones, a process that promises to produce much more favorable outcomes. Developing greater self-awareness also allows us to draw on newfound inner strength and latent potential.

Additionally, as we explore our basic beliefs, we have an opportunity to delve into more profound questions, such as the meaning of life and our place in it. What was I born to do?

As we contemplate these weighty issues, we can discover our true passion, our calling in life, a way to make a difference in the world. Awakening to a deeper truth gives our life purpose and hope, even in the face of a turbulent tempest.

Success Assignment:

As honestly as possible, ask yourself: *What are the most basic beliefs that I hold about others and myself?*

Two of my most fundamental beliefs are as follows:

- I am 100 percent responsible for my life and for my happiness. No one else can provide happiness to me, and it rests on no one else's shoulders to give me my happiness, period. End of story.
- I live in a world of infinite possibilities. Life holds the promise of countless potential outcomes at any moment. I can exert my free will and take personal responsibility to explore as many alternatives as I choose. This allows me to live with a sense of true freedom and empowerment.

Because of these two fundamental beliefs, I have found enormous room to explore every option available when I am feeling vulnerable. At these times, I take a deep breath before reacting to change. Above all, instead of just becoming fearful or angry, I take a step back before I act, which allows me to change gears and become "curious."

Curiosity gives us time to examine our assumptions. It is very rare that reality is reflected by what appears on the surface. Curiosity also gives us time to examine whether we are projecting old fears and grudges onto the current situation; that is, whether we are running old tapes that may be clouding our judgment. By becoming inquisitive rather than upset, we are able to keep perspective and clarify our needs and wants in any given situation.

Rather than considering Change to be an end, view it as a time for a new beginning. Transitions provide an ideal opportunity for us to take a deep look at our life, where we have been and where we are headed. Life really is too short and precious to defer our dreams. Change gives us the chance to seize the moment, change direction if necessary and make a positive transformation that can last a lifetime.

This is the crux of my definition of Spirit.

Life is to be enjoyed. I love just about every minute of mine. My desire is for everyone to be able to make that statement.

In the pages that follow I will share some specific exercises and strategies that can assist anyone in taking the helm and steering a new course toward a rewarding and prosperous future.

If we do our best to pursue a healthy mind, body. and spirit, we can increase our vitality, expand our self-awareness and develop the skills we will need to become the most capable Captain of our ship, *"Living Well During Times of Change."*

Care for the Spirit

- ☐ Happiness Is a Choice, Not an Outcome
- ☐ Care for Others
- ☐ The Nature of Prayer
- ☐ Embrace Your Anchors

I do not consider Spirituality to be purely about one's religion. I think of it as the caring and contemplative side of our nature that seeks to grasp the meaning of life and extends compassion to all of humanity. Of course, religion may be a component of that, but even a walk on the beach or a trip to an art gallery can put us in touch with the cosmic grandeur of all that is.

We use the word "Love" to describe a feeling we have for another person or thing. Even though the word 'Love' remains the same, the sensation that is being experienced by everyone may vary greatly. But as imprecise as language may be to describe things we are unable to measure or explain intellectually, it is the only means we should reach shared meaning and mutual understanding. The Spirit falls in this same realm.

Psychologist Dr. Elisabeth Kubler-Ross, in her book *On Death and Dying*, lists common events, universally shared events in our lives that can trigger intense emotions. The list includes:

- The death of someone close to us
- The realization of our own impending death
- Marriage
- The birth of a child
- Divorce
- The Empty Nest (the kids are gone)
- Relocating (moving from one home to another)
- Changing jobs

The common denominator to all these universal events is: **Going from the Known to the Unknown.**

If you find yourself experiencing one or more of these stressors, give yourself a break. You don't have to behave perfectly. You don't get extra points for acting as if you are the epitome of strength and bravery, only more stress. A far more useful approach during uncertain times is to pause and reflect– to get in touch with what your heart says, not just your mind.

In the next few pages, I share some of my ideas on how best to enhance our spiritual side, in the pursuit of contentment and serenity in **times of Change**.

But, it all starts with a view of the root of *life's purpose*: **Happiness – pure and simple.**

CHAPTER 4

Happiness Now– Happiness for a Lifetime

Happiness Is a Choice, Not an Outcome

IF ANY OF us thought we had only a brief time left to live, we would live every single day as though it were our last, and do everything possible to make each moment count. Adopting this spirit for a lifetime will result in the most joy-filled and worthwhile existence imaginable.

This is it! It comes down to today. Yesterday is gone. Tomorrow is not yet here. But today, this moment, you can treasure the beauty and bounty all around and move ever closer to your dream, NO MATTER WHAT MAY

OCCUR! If you live only in the past or constantly fret about the future, your life passes you by while you miss the power of now.

It all boils down to our beliefs, and our attitudes. We can *choose* whether we will let someone or something bring us down or avert us from our goals. It's the old glass half-full, half-empty principle, so simple, but so true. If we train our minds to see the opportunities and possibilities in *any* situation, rather than just the obstacles and problems, we realize that happiness is our choice, not just a possible "outcome."

I have observed this phenomenon repeatedly. For instance, in working closely with groups who, for example, have been informed that their job has evaporated, I find there is always quite a disparity in reactions. Some people panic and feel emotionally devastated, while others see the turn of events to be a terrific opportunity to explore new options.

It would be far too easy to dismiss this dichotomy as merely the product of the differences in financial, family, or labor market circumstances. But I have not found this to be the case. What I *have* observed is that, by and large, pessimists feel overwhelmed by change whereas optimists feel energized.

We must look inside ourselves to find the fundamental cause of our happiness or unhappiness. Realizing we *can* choose, every day on a conscious level, how we will feel that day sets us free in the most profound sense.

Say the following daily promise aloud every morning– (quietly of course because you are the only one who needs to hear this, and you do!):

Today, just for today, I will have a GREAT day. This will be the BEST DAY OF MY LIFE... bar none, and for all time.

Saying daily this promise to yourself becomes a pledge, a solemn oath. You may have days when you backslide, sure. But over time you will notice your days are filled with appreciation and exhilaration.

This should be reduced to a moment-to-moment endeavor, as well. In other words, each of my days consists of a series of hours, minutes, and, of course, experiences. As each moment goes by, I am experiencing *something*. As each moment passes, I try to **pay attention** to the unfolding moment and look at the experience with a wondering set of eyes.

I affirmatively work to **appreciate** what I am experiencing, in-the-moment. If I am driving in the car, I try to focus on my driving, of course, but on route to my destination, there are trees, people, and all sorts of other observable phenomenon on my journey. I allow myself to wonder at these and **notice them**, as though this could be my very last minute on this earth – in which case I'd want to cherish these moments and observations in the most powerful way that I can. Buddhists call this *Mindfulness*.

I highly recommend a discipline of orienting to our world to **enjoy** every moment (hence, every day and every week, and so on) to the fullest.

I'll write more about the concept of *Appreciation* a little later.

My Experience

For many years, I was a profoundly unhappy person. I believed that I was totally alone in this world and that no one understood what I was feeling. Every day was a painful experience. My friends and family tiptoed around me, afraid to say anything for fear of how I might react.

Then, some years ago, I had the tremendous good fortune to be told about the Affirmation above. I was told that it would reverse my sense of being a victim I had lived with most of my life. This wonderful person told me to stop feeling sorry for myself, that every one of us has problems and that no one thinks others really understand their pain. I trusted this bold and plainspoken woman who encouraged me to take charge of my life. She told me to repeat the above Affirmation every single morning, adding that I didn't have to believe in its power for it to have an effect, that everybody "fakes it" at first.

She promised that the day would come when I would realize that my life had been completely transformed by the process.

She also suggested that I consider practicing Buddhism. She explained it was a powerful tool that could be used to achieve happiness and would supplement the impact of the Affirmation because both are based on the premise that everyone creates his or her own destiny with their words, thoughts, and deeds.

Without question, the combination seemed formidable. I asked her how long it might take– in the worst-case scenario– just so she would know I wasn't committing to do this for the rest of my life.

She replied that she knew many people who had made this practice a part of their lives, and that not a single one had failed to reap rich rewards for their effort. She added that it usually took no more than three months for anyone that she encountered to appreciate the effect.

So, I made a commitment to myself to try both for a period of one hundred days, adding a few days for good measure. I decided that if it hadn't worked in that amount of time, I would quit. I had nothing to lose, and if nothing else, I might get some small pleasure in proving her wrong.

A couple of times I missed a day. I would forget or get distracted. To keep my experiment honest, I would begin a hundred-day cycle all over again. Well, that was nearly thirty years ago. To this very day, I Affirm every single morning. I must say that her promise was completely fulfilled.

Every day of my life is filled with joy and wonder. I feel as though I am the most fortunate person on the planet. I take the good things that occur as thrilling pleasures and the negative as challenges that provide opportunities for growth and enrichment, never taking one moment for granted.

In summation: many people delude themselves into believing that happiness is an outcome, a destination. Evidence of this view is clear when you hear phrases like, "As soon as I find a mate, I'll be happy." Or "When I'm wealthy, I'll be happy." "If only my spouse would stop (fill in the blank), then I could be happy." This erroneous belief brings about a great deal of misery because people feel powerless to direct their destiny. In fact, it is and always has been within our control to DECIDE how we will feel.

Success Assignment: You don't believe me? That's normal. Healthy skepticism is the sign of a probing mind. But, just in case I am correct, just in case my experience is not an isolated case, would it hurt to try this Affirmation? With nothing to lose and everything to gain, repeat the words of the Affirmation every morning for one hundred days. Your life will be forever changed at the end of that time and you will feel happier than ever before.

Today, just for today, I will have a WONDERFUL day. This will be the BEST DAY OF MY LIFE... bar none, and for all time.

Care For Others

When we practice kindness and compassion for others, we enrich and redeem our own lives. Selfishness limits our existence whereas altruism expands it. Helping others enables us to keep our problems in perspective. From an even broader point of view, when we care for others, we benefit ourselves because all life is interconnected, like a gigantic universal web. If one section is harmed, the entire web of life is impacted. Or as the saying goes, "What goes around comes around."

But let's also be clear that care for another does not imply that that person is no longer responsible for his or her own happiness and wellbeing.

Success Assignment: Try this affirmation every day: "What I do in my job, in my family and in my community, *I will do for the sake of others* so that others will be able to learn to care for themselves. I dedicate my activities this day to their success and happiness."

The Nature of Prayer

I consider prayer a way to get in touch with the core of my soul, the most noble, wise and gracious part of my self, along with the power and love inherent in the cosmos.

When I pray, I try to tap the best qualities in the universe and in myself. I think of my prayers as **prayers of promise,** a promise to live up to my highest potential and to make a difference in the world. When I pray in this way I can harness unlimited life force and insight for **I am absolutely convinced that sincere prayer reaps visible rewards.**

I do not believe that prayer should be *a request* for outside intervention because, to me, that approach implies humans are powerless and incapable, something I find impossible to believe. Even when a prayer is directed to God, I feel it is important that one remain an active participant in the process of attaining the desired result.

At a time of radical Change, prayer provides powerful support and solace. Your form of prayer is likely to be very different from mine, but the manner is not important, only the underlying spirit. So, if your prayer has slipped into mere habit or has become a rarity performed only in the presence of others, *now is a perfect time to reflect and begin anew.*

So many of my clients have found inspiration and tapped profound inner strength as the result of their prayer, a strength that has allowed them to persevere and ultimately win during times of Change.

I will be praying for your success and happiness. I hope you will, too.

Embrace Your Anchors

Change causes upheaval; the norm has been disrupted, so it's easy to feel disoriented and insecure. Many people lose confidence in themselves and in the future with so many uncertainties and ambiguities arising.

One of my clients had a very fitting description for her circumstances, in her experience undergoing Change. She said, emotionally, she felt as though she was trying to stand on a waterbed with an elephant constantly rolling around on the other end.

At times like these we crave certainty and stability, we need to hold onto something solid. I call these intangible things "Anchors" because they provide a sense of security and safety. Here is a partial list, by no means exhaustive.

- The relationship with our mate
- The love of our children
- Our religious or spiritual beliefs
- Our friendships
- Our extended family's love and support

- Our adoring pets
- Our talents– what makes us unique and special
- Our knowledge and wisdom
- Our experiences– what we have accomplished
- Our sense of humor
- Our interests

These are the kinds of things that serve as a safe harbor during the storm. Just as a sailor knows he will be secure when he drops anchor, our own "Anchors" provide comfort and protection. We can always depend on these gifts, if we continue to nurture and appreciate them. Indeed, our anchors are our greatest treasures of all.

The thirteenth century Buddhist priest, Nichiren, wrote, *"The greatest treasures of all are the treasures of the heart."*

How do I get to a place of Happiness?

It is only through mastery of the traits described below that we can reach a level of genuine self-awareness and confidence that is unshakable. This is truly what Living Well means.

☐ Take 100% responsibility
☐ Replace anger with curiosity.
☐ Live in the present.
☐ Persevere.
☐ Know yourself.

Take 100% Responsibility

A common view in society is the belief that outside forces are responsible for our problems. Taking personal responsibility goes against the grain in our society. Generally, people tend to blame outside factors for their misery, maybe the boss, or a spouse, or the government, you name it.

One definition of insanity I have heard is: repeating the same behavior repeatedly but expecting a different outcome.

Someone else's behavior is not within our power to control, so it is a futile proposition to try to change others. The only power we truly possess is the ability to control our own actions.

If someone behaves badly, it is their problem; they must deal with the consequences of their actions. So rather than *wasting a minute of your precious time in your precious life wrestling with why people act the way they do, it would be far wiser to put your efforts into discovering the triggers you possess that keep you from effectively dealing* with those causing you so much distress.

When we consciously change our view to take ownership of the events in our lives, we expend our energy in a positive way, using it to identify the options available. We then free ourselves from the role of "victim."

For instance, if we are told we are going to be terminated from a job, instead of lashing out at the management, it is in our own best interest to center our energy on planning an effective course of action. In this way, we become the Navigator in our journey, charting a successful course through the sea of this Change.

Let's be clear: There is no such thing as a problem-free existence, so don't exhaust yourself fretting, just explore and discover a new route to your goals in this adventurous, un-charted territory.

Success Assignment: The next time you hear yourself thinking that someone else's actions have affected you in some way, step back and ask yourself: "What can I do differently to remain happy and in control of my life? If I try a different approach or response, can I create a different result?"

As one of my professors, Edith Seashore at Johns Hopkins University, used to recommend: **"Replace anger with curiosity"**. It was invaluable advice.

To be able to take 100% responsibility, we cannot let ourselves get carried away by our emotions.

A very effective way to stop our emotions from escalating is to put on the curiosity brakes.

Curiosity allows us to switch gears and slow down, providing enough time to get to the heart of the matter.

Anger puts us off course; curiosity gives us time to study the map.

This technique provides a fantastic mechanism to avoid mishaps, a sharp word that can never be taken back or a rash move that is irreversible. Once we decelerate, we can make a deliberate decision about which direction to head in on our journey.

Live in the Present

Isn't it the case that our emotions about a present situation are deeply affected by our past experiences and future hopes?

Certainly, when pretty much anything occurs in our life, we react to this thing due, in large part, to its familiarity ("Oh, here we go again" "This is just like so many things in the past and they turned out badly [or, OK]". Because of this associative reaction, we tend to judge the current moment through a lens of history, as though all things that seem similar, must be the same. I think that this is how we get ourselves into trouble, so often.

In fact, even identical things that happen to each of us will not necessarily have the identical outcome. This is because,

I believe, <u>our reaction</u> (how we respond) to any turn of events is the predictive factor in how the event turns out.

Let me give another business example.

Years ago, I was told by an employer that my services were no longer required. I was immediately devastated by this event. It was due to a decision that I made during my job that had caused a stakeholder to become very angry and express this anger to my boss. My boss, in turn, was already in trouble with his boss and didn't want another customer complaint to go "upstairs" about our department. As a result, I, the newest employee, was given the boot. Ironically, I have always believed that the statement that I had made to our customer was correct. Yet, I was not given the opportunity to explain my "side", just fired immediately and publicly.

Now, this action of being fired threw me for a loop. I had just rented an apartment in a new city to be close to the job and I had very little in the way of savings. There was no severance pay offered and no positive reference to use for a new job prospect.

I spent several days in a depressed "funk". I was reluctant to tell my parents or friends about what had happened. This was a very low point in my young life.

Quite a few years later, I was a senior Human Resources executive with a medium sized company. I had only been at the job for about a year when the company was sold to a large competitor.

I learned during the acquisition period that the buying company already had a Human Resources Officer and that she would continue in that role for the now larger combined company. I spoke with several executives of the buying company and they confirmed that I would be out of a job once the merger was completed – several months later.

As was natural, I was troubled by this prospect. Now I was older and, I thought, less likely to be hired into a similar position.

But I made the decision to keep my head down and focused on my job and the well-being of all the employees for whom I had responsibility.

I certainly did send my resume to other companies, explaining in the cover letter that I would be available after the merger date.

In the meantime, I continued to encourage my fellow executives to do their best, and most were indeed hired by the new company.

Just before the purchase of our company was completed, my boss called me into his office. He reminded me that the company being acquired had added some stocks for me as part of my "hiring bonus" and he asked me to sign them over as part of the purchase transaction. Of course, I agreed but asked if he knew what the value of a share would be once the purchase was final.

He said that the value of the stocks that I was selling to the new company were now valued at a fantastic new amount and totaled several hundred thousand dollars (they were worth only a few thousand when given to me when I originally accepted the job). I was very happy about this, but I knew that I might have to use much of it (after taxes) to live until the next job might come along.

One week before the closing of the deal (and end of my job) two things happened.

One was that I was counseled by the new company's Human Resources Officer that I was being offered a very generous severance package of six months of my salary and a termination bonus. I accepted all.

The other thing that happened was that I got a phone call from a recruiter for a Fortune 100 company. He said that his client was looking for a Vice President of Human Resources who had experience with Mergers and Acquisitions.

Long story short, I was offered that new job at a salary almost twice my current one with a "sign on bonus" of six months of pay.

Well, this second job termination story in my life had a very different ending than the first, didn't it?

The key take-away here is that virtually the same thing occurred as at my job early in my business life. I lost my job.

But, in the latter case, I chose to see that the turn of events offered possibilities. I could pick myself up and realize that there was just as much likelihood that I would fail as that I would prosper.

On the fear of failure side, I was, like most people, fearful because of my experience from earlier in life. *__It was natural to be influenced by events of the past__*. But I chose to set those aside and "work the problem". Indeed, fear paralyzes all of us at times. I **chose** to not let this happen. I am delighted by the outcome.

And here I will add that *our assumptions about the future will often impact how we react* to events in our lives.

At the time of the merger, I was in my late 50's. I was already contemplating my future years of an enjoyable retirement where there would be plenty to do and sufficient funds to afford a comfortable life. These were the future images that I was tempted to allow to influence how I felt about losing an excellent job late in life.

But, again, I set those thoughts aside. I did this <u>consciously.</u>

Here's the thing. I choose to live in the here and now – today. I'll write about this again later. But, let me say that I know that the PAST is just that – past. It is gone and I can't change a thing about it.

On the other hand, the future is not here yet. So, why spend my time dreaming about what <u>might be</u>, and pay attention to what **is** happening and surrounding me in my life **<u>right now</u>**?

Yes, the past is gone and the future just isn't here yet. But I have this moment. This one. Right now, sitting at my desk, enjoying my writing while sitting comfortably in my den while dinner is cooking in the next room and smelling terrific.

This moment. This one right now. This will never come again. I do not want to miss all that exists in my moment that gives pleasure and joy. This is my life. Right now. Right here. Nowhere else. No other time. If I am to be happy, it must be right now, right here. This moment. This one – is the absolute most important moment of all, regardless of what has preceded and no matter what comes tomorrow. Because I have this – this one – the most important and happiest of all moments.

And now THIS one is… and so forth and so forth…

Learn Perseverance

We can always begin again.

I have had my fair share of things in life that didn't turn out nearly as successfully as I had hoped. In fact, fifteen years ago the company I was had started went bankrupt because of a major error in judgment on my part. I was forced to fight my way back from homelessness. I personally guaranteed every obligation of the company, which drained me of all my resources, but eventually I came back. Like so many people before me, I picked myself up, dusted off my very battered ego, swallowed a whole lot of pride, and got a job and then another and since then I have never stopped advancing.

I know now *I can always come back!* In this sense, I am now invincible. You are no different.

A necessary characteristic of the most successful job seeker is perseverance. This is the indomitable spirit of those who will not accept silence from a prospective employer or defeat in the face of rejection. The successful job seeker is proactive; he or she does not sit at home and wait for the phone to ring as though all the responsibility lies with the employer to stay in touch. Indeed, the squeaky wheel does often get the oil.

It is not unusual for some time to go by before the new job offer comes, even if someone exerts a tremendous amount of effort. Please know that, in more than twenty years of working with people with just this job-change challenge, **EVERYONE EVENTUALLY FOUND A JOB IF HE OR SHE DID NOT GIVE UP.** One hundred percent is not a bad average. This statistic should be pretty encouraging to anyone who is faced with the need to seek new employment.

We have all heard many stories of people who have picked themselves up and started over. Here's an incredible example of someone who was unwilling to let failure defeat them. Abraham Lincoln, who faced daunting obstacles throughout his life went on to become one of America's greatest presidents.

Abraham Lincoln

Lincoln lost his job in 1832.
He was defeated for state legislature in 1832.
He failed in business in 1833.
He was elected to the state legislature in 1834.
His sweetheart died in 1835.
He had a nervous breakdown in 1836.
He was defeated for Speaker in the state legislature in 1838.
He was defeated for nomination for Congress in 1843.
He was elected to Congress in 1846.
He was again defeated for nomination for Congress in 1848.
He was rejected for land officer in 1849.
He was defeated for U.S. Senate in 1854.
He was defeated for nomination for Vice President in 1856.

Again he was defeated for U.S. Senate in 1858.
Abraham Lincoln was elected President in 1860.

President Abraham Lincoln's experience should give anyone inspiration that nothing is impossible as long as we *never give up*.

So, if the change that is occurring in your life right now seems like a setback, think of it instead as a starting point to launch a new expedition towards the life of your dreams, a time to find new opportunity and explore new possibilities.

- True success in life comes to the navigator, never to the victim.
- A navigator never gives up; he or she perseveres until the destination is reached.
- A navigator sees his or her responsibility and challenge to stay afloat and remain on course.
- A navigator knows there will always be stormy waters during the voyage but that by taking charge the ship can ride the waves and reach the other shore.

Your Personal Identity (Know Yourself)

I think the way in which we refer to ourselves reveals a tremendous amount about our self-image, and whether we see ourselves as Victims or as Navigators.

Navigators normally refer to themselves in professional and highly positive terms, no matter what their current employment status may be.

To illustrate this: Think about someone you have known who lost a job and spent some time before gaining new employment.

How did he or she refer to themselves in social situations? This may seem like a subtle point but can make a dramatic difference in our life experience.

Did they refer to themselves as being "unemployed"? Or did they say, "I am a Banker or Lawyer"?

Note the difference. It is enormous. The first response is certainly accurate, but the person is identifying themselves in negative terms. There is a permanent sound to it.

Language is important. The phrasing we use to describe ourselves reaches our psyche, our soul. At least in part, other people form opinions about us by relying on the "messages" we relay to them. We don't want the listener to think we are somehow flawed or that we are seeking sympathy. It is far more effective to put forth a confident and purposeful image.

Case Study: A Story That Hits Home

I can tell you of an instance a few years ago when someone approached me after a workshop to speak privately with me. She told me that her husband had been unemployed for more than a year and that he was not even trying anymore. She said that this was financially devastating for the family, as they required dual incomes to support their needs.

I immediately asked her how her husband would describe himself in a social situation. She said *that he always* referred to himself as unemployed.

I then told her about my observation that the way we portray ourselves to others reflects our self-image, which in turn determines to a substantial extent the type of responses we receive from those in our environment.

I asked her to have her husband call me, and she said that she would insist that he do so. When he called that evening, I invited him to meet with me the next day.

As I had expected, he essentially had given up hope of finding another job. He had experienced a few close calls early in his job search but had not been selected. Of course, this had been deeply painful. Like most of us, he was reluctant to be hurt again.

That's the irony of <u>pain avoidance</u>. The surest way to avoid being hurt is to choose not to play. It really works. The problem though, is that in the end we experience even more pain by evading the initial challenge. Then it becomes a vicious cycle, which if carried out to the extreme would lead to complete immobility and seclusion – not a very promising strategy to employ for success.

The man was aware of this, of course, but he didn't realize just how deeply the rejection had affected him. He sincerely wanted to reverse the current situation but just wasn't sure about the next step. So I advised him to do several things.

First, I asked him to cease referring to himself as "unemployed." He selected a phrase that described what he wanted to do, and he practiced saying that phrase to me until I felt confident it was rolling off his tongue rather easily.

Then I asked him to make a commitment to do one other thing.

I told him to get a job.

That's it. It was just that simple.

I told him to get a job by five o'clock the next day. He protested, of course, thinking that I was joking. I told him that he could do it if he made up his mind and set a clear deadline for himself. I pointed out that this job could be something for the interim. It didn't have to be the job that would last him a lifetime (Does anyone have such a thing anymore anyway?) but that he must decide to have a job by the next afternoon. I didn't even tell him how to accomplish this. I knew that he was fully capable of figuring it out.

The gentleman called me the next evening to report that he had accepted a night audit job in a small hotel. I congratulated him. All work is honorable!

The gentleman in this story had been an architect previously. In this new position, he would be working "behind the scenes" where he didn't have to worry about being recognized, if that was a concern. And, he would work evening hours, so he still had the bulk of the day to search for an architect's position. But he would do so from a greater position of strength, at least in his own <u>sense of self-worth</u>.

I received a brief note in the mail just a month later from his wife. She thanked me for energizing her husband to break out of his cycle of failure. And she wanted to let me know that he had accepted a full-time position as a senior architect at the largest firm in their county at a much higher rate of pay than he had dared hope for or ever received before.

She seemed quite impressed with my coaching. You now know the principles that I applied to his situation. I asked him to *"decide to stop being a Victim and start being a Navigator."* I insisted that he be as *specific* as possible in stating his goal and to include for himself a time limit. I told him to change his *vocabulary* as to how he referred to himself, and, in the end, he took *full responsibility* for the great and positive outcome that was just around the corner.

He is truly a "FIRST CLASS PERSON," in my view.

PART TWO

Our Place In The World Of Work After Age 65

CHAPTER 5

The Buggy Whip Reality

- ☐ The last Buggy Whip manufacturer
- ☐ The Past was great, but, that was THEN and THIS IS NOW
- ☐ Everything CHANGES, ALWAYS
- ☐ CHANGE is neither "Good" nor "Bad" nor "Right" nor "Wrong"
- ☐ Bottom Line: It doesn't matter what any change is in my life. All that matters is how I RESPOND to that Change – now THAT allows me to be happy, or not

The Last Buggy Whip Manufacturer

You may have heard this story before, but it is worth a retelling to consider our handling of Change in our lives.

The story is a metaphor, of course, and it goes like this:

Somewhere around 1910 in America, somewhere in a North-Eastern State, one of the last company's producing primarily whips for horse drawn carriages (they were called "Buggy Whips") was slowly winding down production every month. Sales had gone down dramatically – people just weren't buying buggy whips anymore, or so it seemed.

Around this time, all the competitors of this company were either shutting down or changing their product lines to seek a demand.

But the owner of this company refused to change. He told his dwindling workforce that this must be a temporary slump and if they (his company) could just hold out for a bit longer, they stood to make a fortune when demand reignited.

He was sure that it would.

In fact, an often-retold story about this company owner recalls that one morning the owner was standing outside of the front door of his business having a smoke with a trusted employee.

As they stood there together, a Ford Model T drove by on the unpaved street, making a lot of noise and emitting foul smelling fumes.

The owner of the buggy whip business smiled and said confidently to his associate, "Well, there's your proof! This new gadget (the automobile) will NEVER CATCH ON. It's just a flash in the pan. It's just too noisy and fumes from its engine are terrible. It'll never be as reliable as a horse. No, Sir. This is obviously just a fad. We'll wait it out and we'll be winners!"

Well, **we all know how that prediction turned out**. I'm sure that, over a century later, automobiles are here to stay. At least until the next mode of personal transportation comes to market… and then the next one after that … and so forth.

Oh, and although there is a market for whips, there are no longer companies manufacturing them as a sole product.

Well, here's the meaning of this metaphor for me:

It's quite human to want to hold on to the familiar and avoid the murky unknown. And since this leads to a cautiousness, it's not necessarily a terrible thing. But, the trick to success, is acknowledging our fears about things that are "new", and then cautiously finding our new reality where we can capitalize on Change and not be harmed by it.

At some point, we each must let go of things with which we are familiar and venture into current ways of behaving. But, still, doing so with caution.

Here's an example of this sense of caution.

Like most seniors in our society, I have watched in awe the rapid evolution of gadgets that allow diverse ways to communicate – from simple cell phones to Skype.

I've been flustered many times by the rapidly changing technologies and by how quickly the population will adopt the newest version of whatever is popular.

At this writing, I have a cell phone, but it only receives phone calls – nothing written – nothing else. I have had to do some arm twisting among some of my family members in this regard.

Some of my nieces and nephews, and one grandson, have tried several times to send a text message to me, though I have set my phone to send them an immediate return message stating that my phone does not accept text messages. It goes on to tell the would-be communicator that if they have something to convey to me, they are to call me on my home phone line and speak directly to me. Anything short of that will not merit a response.

You see, I just don't care what the rest of society is doing in this communication realm. <u>I have elected to not participate,</u>

and I feel good about that decision. I will hold out, even amidst the criticisms of those who dare to voice them (to me).

I consider this to be maintaining my power and individuality in an area of my choice.

However, I realized some time ago that I must learn and utilize other forms of communications to make my way in the world. The Internet is a tool that I choose to participate in for many things such as purchasing common items and staying current with world developments. And, many colleagues and acquaintances relay heavily on this medium to share information and set meetings.

So, I am picking and choosing the new media that fits my needs and temperament. I'm deciding what I will make use of only after consideration of usefulness, costs, and time usage. I refuse to rush into use of a tool just because it has become popular.

Here's my determination, based on the buggy whip metaphor.

I am now determined that I will pay close attention to the changes, particularly in technology, that occur.

On the one hand, I will remain wary of the temptation to "jump into" the use of technologies simply because a substantial portion of the population seems to be adopting these new gadgets. To a certain degree, I see this as constituting nothing more than a fad – contrived by the technology companies for increasing their profits.

Haven't you noticed how our fellow citizens use and enjoy their newest electronic device? They will tell us in great length and detail about how fancy and useful the gadget may be for them.

Then, usually in less than a calendar year, those very same associates tell us that they are "over the moon" about the next generation of gadget that has been announced by the technology creators. Our friends will tell us, in detail, how much better, faster, and more useful the updated version promises.

Well, seeing this phenomenon makes me extremely cautious. How can the next generation of any devise be available on the mass market in only a year? Aren't these things developed over time, with research, construction, and trials?

Well, here's how this affects me. I start all considerations from the perspective of what I "need", not just what I "want". And, certainly, I disavow any sense of competition or "keeping up with the Jones'". That is just a waste of my time and money – keeping up, I mean.

My only question is: Do I need the next generation, or the thing itself?

I don't care how smart and pretty the advertisements claim. I only care about utility. And, is my life going to be affected by the modern technology in a way that I NEED?

Back to the Buggy Whip. Certainly, I do not want to be the one left behind by the technology changes, simply because I want to hold on to a past that may not stick around. But, I don't have to see this as a zero-sum game. And, above all, I don't want my life to be influenced too deeply by fads that are devoid of a meaningful difference in my happiness and experience of life.

My recommendation to others is – do the same inventory that I've described above. Please check yourself.

Ask if you are satisfied with the technology that's available to you. Is your life enhanced by the technology?

Is it a burden? Are you down-loading new "apps" and then not using them because what they provide is just not useful to you?

Well, I have asked myself those questions for every "new" tech opportunity that crosses my path.

I have decided this: if I can use it on a consistent basis, I'll go all in and learn and buy what is needed.

However, and above all, I will not let myself be "bullied" into buying and trying to use any new thing that doesn't meet the standard I described above. I won't be influenced by other people's perceptions and about what may have utility for them. I am not them.

Here is the nub of the cultural phenomenon that seems to be creating techno-billionaire people and companies. There is a "hype" that I see in play that entices folks to always rush to get the next generation and newest version of any technology that they are using. This phenomenon seems to keep people (mostly younger people) with a bit less money in their pockets and spending a whole lot more time "fidgeting" with devices for no apparent reason.

So, yes, this is going on all around us older folk. I've noticed that youngsters have given themselves permission to be entertained by those of us who do not share the popular hysterias. It may not have occurred to them that it is THEM who are entertaining because they desire more and better technology without an attendant benefit worthy of the money and time that they invest.

The Past was great, but, that was THEN and THIS IS NOW

The SWEET MEMORY PHENOMENON

This is one of the most common causes of unhappiness for so many people that I have met – and sometimes, for me, too.

Failing to remember the above reality causes this:

We can easily find ourselves with our memories of times that are past. And, so often, the memories of those days of our youth (or last year, too) can be so pleasant. We smile remembering how things used to be and remember all the enjoyment of those days and experiences.

While in such a luxuriating memory time, we very often find ourselves forgetting the difficulties of those days and remembering only the parts that we found to be peaceful and enjoyable.

Very often, don't we conflate the happiness that we are remembering in any given set of past events or days?

It's just more fun to put the parts of any memory that caused us stress and displeasure into a mental closet. We would just rather not look at those aspects of a memory since it would lessen or negate the rich enjoyment of the good parts of any experience.

I am certainly not willing to say that there is anything wrong or "bad" with selective memories – where the unpleasant aspects of the memories are ignored completely and only the fun and comforting aspects of the memories are recollected. No, this can be positive and serve to relax us in the here and now.

But, what may be delightful in small doses (remembering events through a sweet lens) can morph into a habit of fanciful re-writing of history – the beginning of one's break with REALITY. Again, this is often positive in small doses where we know, deep down, that we are selectively parsing the memory to cleanse it of sour pieces and focusing only on the best of the memory.

And this brings us to the potentially destructive part of the **SWEET MEMORY PHENOMENON.**

It seems clear to me now that as many of us (I am included) age, we are so often prone to look back – nostalgically – on our past and spend much time reveling in the remembered goodness of days gone by.

Yet, the reality is that we are not living THEN, we are living NOW.

And here's the "AHA" that I've had on this point:

All the time that I spend reminiscing about years ago, there is a world of life and experiences that surround me at the same moment. Oh, and most definitely there is JOY in the here and now, if I choose to see it.

MINDFULNESS

"Life is a dance. Mindfulness is witnessing that dance."
— Amit Ray, Mindfulness:
Living in the Moment - Living in the Breath

*"Let go of your mind and then be mindful.
Close your ears and listen!"*
— Jalaluddin Rumi, Love's Ripening: Rumi on the Heart's Journey

"Be happy in the moment, that's enough. Each moment is all we need, not more."
— Mother Teresa

Buddhists have taught a concept called, **Mindfulness**.

In its essence, MINDFULNESS means the conscious experiencing of each moment of life as it unfolds. It means that nothing is trivial and we are best served by PAYING ATTENTION, without judgement – to every moment and every event of our lives. This is easier said than done. I, for one, work at this, though because I desire the richness and fabric that this adds in every moment of my life.

CHAPTER 6

Technology Challenges

HERE'S A REAL challenge for all of us. Doesn't it seem that just when we master the latest program or form of technology, another version has come into use and the version that we have just learned is considered obsolete?

Well, I applaud the manufacturers of these waves of technology who relentlessly produce a newer technology while the previous version is still on the sales shelf.

I see the trick here.

I suspect that newer versions of things have facets that are only new to the users, but the manufacturers probably invented each rendition long before release.

Sure. What a great sales strategy. This creates an inexhaustible demand for new sales of products that, it seems to me, are only marginally better than the versions they replace.

And, have you noticed the phenomenon of customer/ user complicity? I notice this with my own children and grandchildren, particularly when it comes to their portable telephones (that's what I call them – because that is, in the end, what they are – with myriad extras added on…). And, there is a hysteria, in fact, for young folks, in the main, to be able to acquire the very newest version, even when the one that they are now using – you know, the one that only a few months ago they were raving to us about as being the very latest and BEST that there can be.

Then, in the blink of an eye, the next generation of the thing is announced by the manufacturer and foreshadowed to be just a little bit faster, or jump through more hoops than the currently crazed version that a whole generation of (young) folks just could not live and be happy without.

Wow. Staying up with all this hype and rapid change is really, really challenging.

And herein lies the next point I would like to make.

As we age, it is more and more challenging to learn recent technologies, though not at all impossible. This is where a common challenge comes into play for most of us in the 60 plus years of age.

I think that first, we should give serious thought to whether any recent technology will make our lives better, at least in these ways:

- we will be able to do our jobs better
- stay in touch more effectively with loved ones
- or just interact more constructively with the world outside of ourselves.

To me, these are the crucial decision points that FAR outweigh the hype and advertising about something that's coming to market. I have tried very hard to resist things that are new until I can apply the criteria stated above.

And, only when I have concluded that something new to me will benefit me and my life's joy in the ways stated above, I ask the second most important question:

- What will it take for me to learn this recent technology?
- Am I capable of this learning?
- Will I enjoy the process of learning?

Now, I am not suggesting that level of difficulty is a primary decider of my willingness to jump into learning. It really all comes down to the effort – reward calculation.

And, I'll point out again, I will resist the temptation to "follow the crowd" just for the sake of following or being able to claim bragging rights to new equipment, or innovative ways of utilizing the gadgets on the market.

All of this is because I am completely devoted to the notion of milking "joy" out of every remaining moment of my life. I believe that only by employing the six personal questions, above, will I ensure the avoidance of unnecessary additions to my life while pre-qualifying the new "offerings" in my world, molding their adoption to my needs and basing my actions on Value Creation.

CHAPTER 7

Generational Challenges

ONE OF THE differences in the workplace that those of us over 55 find to be a challenge is the presence of co-workers, subordinates, and often bosses who are younger than we are. Why this becomes a problem I'll discuss here, but it is undeniable that there are daily overt and covert clashes that take place due, in the main, to the difference not only in chronological age of our fellow-workers, but also a noticeable (sometimes dramatic) difference in the way we see the world and how we behave in a work situation from those around us.

Let me start with the perceptions about the world of work that tend to vary between generations.

It is often the case that those of us over 55 grew up in a world where there were set rules of workplace behavior.

Those rules included how to dress, the importance of being on time, how to respond to other employees, for the men – how often to shave our faces (daily), and how to communicate with each other. And, of course, the importance of doing whatever is necessary to keep our job – for an entire working career, if possible, earning a pension and the ability to retire in comfort.

Well, by the time we turned 55, we found ourselves surrounded by younger workers who have entirely different values and, for the most part, no rules at all.

Job Longevity

One of the big differences is found in the perspective and valuation of a job and a career as part of an organization. We, the elders, generally look for a feeling of belonging in an employment group and are determined to hold onto our jobs if we can. Younger generations see just about every job as temporary and can't imagine staying in any job for more than one to two years.

This difference leads us older workers to be impatient with what seems to be a lackadaisical attitude and a lack of care as to the younger workers' longevity in their job.

This difference alone causes both overt and covert conflict in the workplace.

Where the real impact of the new mindset regarding workplace talent retention will continue to be one of the greatest challenges for Human Resources professionals for the foreseeable future.

Dressing for Work

Now the difference between generations around dress standards causes an outwardly visible distinction and often causes the elders to have difficulty taking the younger workers seriously.

In fact, though, this kind of a difference has negligible effect on the ability of workers to be competent in their jobs.

But, the way that I made peace with this phenomenon is this: when I, and my contemporaries, came into the work world, we were from a different "cut" than those already doing the work that we came into.

Yes, I was only a couple of months out of the Marine Corps, but I had adopted the dress of my friends at the time. I had gone to the concert at Woodstock, NY and fallen in love with the Peace, Love, and Rock and Roll generation's habits.

I had taken to hitchhiking to get around, even though I had a car. I traded in that nice 1971 red convertible with low mileage for a VW Bus with high mileage and had spent weeks on the roads of America following concerts and visiting friends – old and new.

Then I returned home and realized that the money that I had saved while overseas would only last a little while longer, so I would have to get a job. A local State Job Center clued me into the standards of "dressing for success". I invested in a suit or two, long sleeve shirts, a couple of ties, and, of course, black laced shoes.

I got a job right away and would stay employed for most of my 34-year career.

But, right from the beginning, I know that I, and my generation, pushed the status quo in our jobs in so many ways. At the very least, we questioned EVERYTHING, and the older workers weren't prepared for or comfortable with that.

But, slowly, standards at work changed to accommodate us – the new generation – the Baby Boomers. Solid Blue and Black suits gave way to thin stripes. White shirts evolved to allow more variety. And, men's ties became multi-colored and high fashion, all a shock to the older workers.

And, in time I realized that this is the way change has always taken place. New ideas lead to new acceptances on the part of those who are established in their ways.

This is the on-going story of change in the work place – in all areas conceivable.

So, this evolution is natural and always continues. So, realizing this, I comforted myself with the changes that I saw the younger workers introducing.

These changes are neither "bad" nor "good", "right", nor "wrong". They are simply different. There's no use feeling threatened by these.

But at the same time, I realized that I can pick and choose the "new" fashions and manners at work that I can become comfortable with. Those that I am not OK with, I can find ways to remain myself. And, this authenticity will, eventually, be appreciated by others, in time.

Use of Technology and accompanying Etiquettes

I have seen the rise of technology (software, Applications, and devices) as mostly a good thing that has added a lot of value and stream lined the work world enormously.

And, probably like you, I have worked hard to adapt and adopt the recent technologies through learning and practice. This has certainly paid off. If for no other reason, I noticed that whenever a "downsizing event" has taken place, the first to be laid off have, for the most part, been those with performance issues and, close behind, those who have not kept up with the ever-changing technologies.

Here I should say that I have learned and changed my ways of doing things MANY times over the 34 years of my working life. Heck, in my first job out of the military, the technology that I had to learn was a Telex Machine – remember those? I was working for an international paper company and that was the quickest and most cost-effective way to communicate with other offices – even several at a time.

Well, over the following 30+ years, there were SO many new things that would come out at an ever-accelerating pace. Eventually, it seemed that just as I would feel that I had mastered one system or gadget, a newer and "better" version of that technology would be released by the maker and I'd start learning again.

I will admit, though, that I was better at learning and adapting when I was younger. It came easily in the early days. And, then it got harder and harder for me to get the newest way of doing things and extremely harder to retain what I had learned.

So, I'll bet I'm not the only one in this boat.

But, here's the thing. We all know that the human brain's ability to learn and retain decreases over the years (the precise age that this begins varies widely). So, it is understandable and entirely "normal" to find increasing difficulty with learning new information and processes, as the average human ages. – It just comes with the territory.

But, I would also like to identify another related occurrence that tends to separate many workers by age groups, as it relates to technology. And, this is about Etiquette.

By this I mean, it seems that many, particularly younger, users of modern technology have adopted interpersonal communications habits that are problematic for many of us in the older generations.

Here are some examples:

- Dropping salutations
- "Multitasking" when also communicating with another in person
- Preferring text communication to oral
- Use of Language – Altered Idioms and Forms of Address
- Hats and Underpants

Dropping Salutation courtesies

I have noticed, and found distracting, that those who communicate with me via textual communications (for me this is solely via email) have given themselves permission to ignore the common courtesies that those in my generation grew up to expect.

For example, in a message, long or short, there is no longer a salutation inserted, such as, "Thank you for asking, here's the answer..." or "Hi, Mike, I hope that you are well. I'm writing to you now because...", and the like.

Also, baffling to me, email authors seldom end a communication like we used to. Examples are, "Thank you for thinking about this for me..." or "That's about all on this topic, please let me know your thoughts" or "Have a great day/week/weekend", and so forth.

"Multitasking" when also communicating with another in person

"Multitasking" – Well, honestly, if I never hear that phrase again, it will be too soon. It seems to me that this phrase is used far too liberally and so often it just puts a nice "mask" on behaviors that would be considered rude, if not for this word's use.

So, I can't help but notice that the old, unwritten rules about direct eye contact during personal, one-on-one communications, have laxed to an extraordinary degree. And, this has at least three manifestations.

First, folks are more likely than ever to choose to look down at some hand-held communication device rather than set it aside and engage both orally and physically (eye contact) when communicating with another. I find this enormously distracting.

Second, in group communication moments (workshop, lecture, etc.) younger (usually, but not always) attendees seem to feel that it is perfectly alright to be looking intently at their personal communications device rather than looking at the speaker. As a frequent lecturer, I have found this to be distracting for me as I have a sense that I have lost that person's attention. Not to mention, the memories from my grade school days when teachers made very strong and clear efforts to keep students' attention on the classroom learning.

Preferring Text

And, third, I have noted a reluctance on the part of folks who are growing up in this age of technology communications to converse directly and in person with another, even a peer.

I'm sure that we all have stories about this phenomenon. Many of us have noticed the tendency of technology babies to avoid face-to-face communications, even with friends and family members. Many prefer to communicate electronically, even if the recipient of the communication is in the very same room.

Use of Language – Altered Idioms and Forms of Address

Have you noticed some of the seemingly random (unexplained and unexplainable) changes in the ways folks are choosing to communicate? And, importantly, are you noticing how this makes you feel?

A couple of examples:

Remember when someone said, *"Thank you"* and (we were taught back in school) the correct response was, *"You're Welcome"* (with a smile)? Well, today, when I say, *"Thank you"* to someone, I'm most likely to hear, *"No problem"* … as though I had suggested that **there was a problem** that the reason for my thanking the person must have caused.

And, here's the key point. It makes me feel quite ancient when this happens – almost daily. My natural internal conversation at that moment when someone responds with, *"No problem"*, is to say, "What language do YOU speak? In

English, we all know that the correct response is a gracious, *'You are welcome'* or even *'Not at all'* or something similar".

Another example that seems to occur daily involves respectful ways to address each other. Oh, has that ever relaxed over the last few years.

When I was a Vice President of Human Resources with a Fortune 100 company, I was regularly surprised by the relaxed forms of personal address that employees, particularly younger team members, allowed themselves. And, the few attempts that I made to require more formality were met with dire responses from both my direct report managers and my own manager (the Senior VP).

Of course, I'll never forget the day that I was walking down a hallway and, seeing one of the young folks who worked in the technology group of my division, walking towards me (with the ever-present "ear buds" in the side of his head), I made eye contact and said, "Hello". His response, without taking the earbuds out, was a simple, "Hey, Dude".

Well, I was told later that for nearly an hour afterwards, I could be seen sitting at my desk in my corner office, considering the distance with a shocked look, and saying, "Dude"? "Really?" "Dude"? …

My laughter finally erupted on this point the following weekend when I was at my son's home for dinner and I told the story of the "Dude" salutation. My daughter-in-law pointed out that I was lucky that the young employee didn't refer to me as "Dog" – another popular form of address today.

We all laughed, but internally I shuttered a bit realizing that the evolving discourse is so rough and puts quite a distance between generations, perhaps unintentionally.

Hats and Underpants

Here's one that throws me for a loop.

First, Hats:

When I was growing up the custom was quite clear that hats were to be worn outside and outside only. This would later be reinforced for me when I was in the military where the same custom was rigidly enforced.

Today, that seems to be out the window entirely. I don't just mean that I see men and women coming into the grocery store and continuing to wear hats. No. I marvel at the wide spread disregard for what was once a strict courtesy and now people leave their hats on (most usually baseball caps) while they are inside homes, churches, and, yes, the office.

There is a thought that races through my brain that wonders if so many people just couldn't take the time to wash their hair on this given morning. What other reason could there be, I ask myself.

In my last years in an office job, I had to summon all my consciousness each and every day to keep silent as so many folks around me wore these ball caps indoors and somehow think that this is normal. Well, I guess that it's the "new normal" but that doesn't mean that I am unaffected.

I now spend much of my time delivering lectures at businesses and in university classrooms. I have taught myself to ignore the proliferation of hat wearing. But it certainly is distracting.

And young men's underpants (I never dreamed that I would write a sentence starting with this phrase, but here goes) – when did it become fashionable for young (and sometimes no-so-young men) to wear their trousers so loosely that they appear ready to fall to their ankles at the next stride?

And, as a result, when said male faces away from us, we are treated to the sight of the top band and more of his underpants. This is done without apparent regard for the sensibility of anyone else in their area. And, again, this is such a fashion change that flies in the face of the way that people in my generation were raised. I know that things change, but their underpants? Really? And at work?

So, what of all of this?

Why does any of this matter, you may ask?

I fear that we have now a couple of generations who are growing up with skills that will be inappropriate to conducting meaningful lives where they contribute to the society.

And, my additional fear is that while this transition of style and behavior is evolving, many of us in the Baby Boom generation are experiencing an enormous challenge in communicating and making progress both at the workplace, as well as inter-family.

I can only offer the time worn advice to see what is really taking place, acknowledge and give voice to your observations, and always take a step back to put our observations into the context of Evolution.

In other words, what we see happening is neither "good" nor "bad", "right" nor "wrong". It is simply a natural turn of events to which we adjust our own behavior, ever so slightly, perhaps, to get along in this uncomfortable new world while maintaining our authenticity.

I, often daily, find myself pointing to actions that others are taking for granted as "OK", but I point out, gently, how that behavior impacts me, but I avoid criticism. What I mean is, I don't believe that I have a right to judge others' behavior, but I do have a responsibility to myself to express the behavior's impact and seek a middle ground where we can find meaning and a way forward.

CHAPTER 8

Are We Drawing Lines in the Sand?

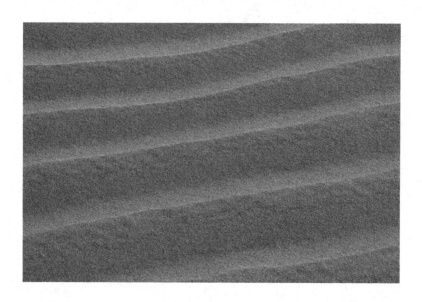

THE PROCESS OF feeling compelled to set a point in any matter beyond which we just will not go can be either very helpful or very self-destructive. This all depends on how we are using this internal control in any given situation.

There are times when this can be quite healthy.

For example, when bombarded with technology options – new gadgets followed rapidly by upgrades and refinements, all of which will cost money that we may or may not be able to afford. This is a situation in which wisdom and valor must be applied.

When we genuinely cannot afford to keep up with the newest of anything, it becomes necessary to be realistic and decide what our budget will be prior to agreeing to upgrade, based on the reality of our financial position.

I have a mobile telephone that is just that – a telephone that seems to work most anywhere. I have not upgraded to the versions of a phone that will replicate the functionality of my computer (emails, Internet searching, taking pictures, and the like). For me, a part of my decision to retire at a somewhat early age (62) necessitated that I will live on a set income and I must be vigilant about how and where I spend money. Vigilant, like never before.

Of course, I pay a price for this thrift. Younger family members have given themselves permission to make fun of my seemingly "old" technology. But, here's the good news. I live within my means and I select technology **with its usefulness TO ME, in mind**. In the end, I must live and manage my life based on rational choices.

The better news is that most of us reach a point in life where we inherently recognize the power of self-management and we can let the uninformed opinions of others just roll off. I, for one, enjoy the comments of others now. In fact, I laugh and enjoy the folly of the judgments of all others, most of which are simply uninformed and, well, just not relevant to my life management.

Although, every now and then, some useful ideas are proffered that I find affordable and useful – making my life management smoother and more enjoyable at a price that I can afford.

Now here's the other side of the coin.

There are temptations that abound for any of us, particularly those of us of a certain age, to draw arbitrary lines in the sand and refuse to reconsider decisions. This is the outward manifestation of a closed mind – very easy to fall into.

Personally, I have decided to review my thinking about most matters throughout this stage of my life with an eye to challenge my assumptions and clarify my motives.

Since it is so improbable to assume that I can be objective when it comes to my own thoughts and decision processes, I have sought counsel from trusted others. I have identified and drawn in a group that I call my "kitchen cabinet" – I know, that phrase is not original.

Well, my kitchen cabinet is a group of six to eight folks, some family members who know me the best, some colleagues, and some just dear and lifelong friends.

I make a point to reach out to this group with regularity and share my thinking in any number of areas (like writing this book). I have asked for absolute honesty and, usually, received it. Most often, the feedback is based on the group's knowledge of me over prolonged periods of time. The feedback is seldom unanimous, and that is quite expected.

All in all, the input of friends and family continues to be my best compass, like a lighthouse in a fog, assisting me to remain grounded and considering my decisions and life course. I cherish them deeply.

PART THREE

Growing Older –
Gracefully (Joyfully)

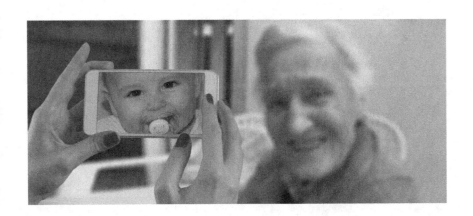

CHAPTER 9

How We See Ourselves

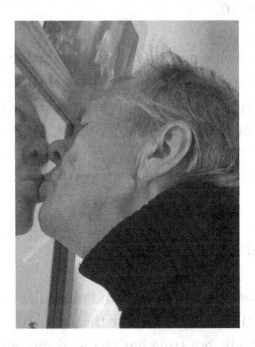

- ☐ What do I see when I look in the mirror?
- ☐ Do I Matter?
- ☐ Am I Valued and Valuable?
- ☐ How do others see me?
- ☐ Do others GAIN from me?
- ☐ What Legacy do I choose to leave behind?

What do I see when I look in the mirror?

This is a critical question for us to ask ourselves all throughout life. I am asking this myself now that I am about to turn 70.

The answer to this question tells me a lot about how I see myself. In the end, that is what I consider crucial rather than comparing myself to some arbitrary conceptions that the world may tell me to measure up to.

Here's the usual answer that I identify.

For the most part, I am delighted with what I see, clothed or unclothed.

No, I don't see the well-shaped and muscular Marine that I was nearly 50 years ago, I figure that I had my days in that image and body, but time has changed me physically and emotionally.

But, here's the thing. The changes that result in how I look today are, in and of themselves, neither good nor bad. I choose to not be comparative, as though a good comparison might make me "happy" with what I see, or the opposite.

No, I have CHOSEN to see myself as the very best "me" that I can be at this moment. I like the guy that I see in the mirror. Although weather-worn, he is a happy and confident human being with lots to give to the world and that's about as good as it gets.

My question to you is: "What do you see when you look in a mirror?"

Now the greatest danger in this is the sum-total of Society's beliefs and messages that tell us a lot about how we should feel, based on what we see in that mirror.

For example, if we are overweight or underweight there is a prescribed meaning and judgement that attend, universally. But that prescription does not equate to "Truth". Well, it might represent Society's Truth, but who says we must sign on to that in the first place?

I, for one, have chosen to acknowledge Society's Truth, but hold myself to my own standards. If I am to be happy for the rest of my days, (and I fully intend to be exactly that) then I must give myself the space to start with, "I am a good person who means well for others, even when imperfect in doing so."

So, my advice is to relax, set Societal standards in their rightful place (nice to know, but I won't let them define me) and fall in love with ourselves – whether for the first time in our lives (better late than never), or to realize again that we are loveable and authentic. The fact seems to be that others will only be able to love me as much as I love me. And that is a critical knowledge.

Give yourself a break. None of us is the picture of anyone else's "perfection", and, at the same time, we are not "Evil Incarnate", no matter how an "Ex…" might characterize us ☺.

When looking in the mirror, I smile. I poke myself in my incredibly large belly and, often, say, out loud, "Ho, Ho, Ho". Why not. I am who I am and I am a good person only because I have DECIDED that I am.

This, of course, is a key point of distinction from my outlook and that of many others.

Other people can see me, but they only do so through the lens of their experiences, layered with their preconceived notions. In other words, when another person makes a judgement about me, they are only expressing their own limited point-of-view. Their view does not constitute objective Truth. Of this, I am now quite certain.

In this spirit, I welcome all feedback from others, but always with my view that what the other person tells me, directly or indirectly, is simply what they see – colored by their own values and life experiences.

So, really, self-evaluation ultimately comes down to me. And any judgement of what I am putting out to the world, is, in the end, solely for me to characterize.

I know that this sounds like an ego-centric view that ignores the judgements of others and that if a fair assessment.

However, I think that the views of others constitute data that I must weigh and factor as I judge my own intentions and actions.

In the end, I am the sum of my judgements about myself, while considering the feedback from others.

So, I must DECIDE how to value myself and define myself. It has taken me nearly 70 years to arrive at this certainty and I am enormously grateful to view myself in a positive and meaningful light.

Do I Matter?

These last four questions are among the most valuable for all of us, well, throughout life. But as we reach senior status, these questions take on a monumental importance.

My life was changed forever when I read a book in college by Dr. Victor Frankl, Jewish/German neurologist and psychiatrist as well as a Holocaust survivor. That book, *"Man's Search for Meaning"*, has been one of the most influential bodies of thought and observation about the truth of my/our existence.

Dr. Frankl observed that at the root of all the layers of what makes each of us who we are is the notion of Meaning. Who are we? What do we stand for? Can we define the reason for being alive?

In this spirit, I am convinced that the fuel for a happy Retirement is to **_Live with a PURPOSE!_** Everyday have a plan and "**Create Value**". I'll share more on this later.

The notion of "making a difference", of being needed and living with purpose are the very core of the design of a happy and rich life as we age.

Am I Valued and Valuable?

This is one of the most critical questions to ask ourselves to pave the way for purposeful living as we age. This is tricky because the answer to this question has been well defined as we were successful and capable in our jobs and felt marginally competent as a parent, child, sibling, and other family member.

So, this was "cooked in" to our many roles throughout our growing years and adulthood.

But as an elder, there are fewer automatic judgement points due to the lack of work involvement and a new role as we have aged within the family structure.

To really answer the Value question, it is necessary to ponder these questions, as well:

How do others see me?
and
Do others GAIN from me?

I became convinced a long time ago that assessing the impact of my life and actions on other folks is one way to gauge how meaningful my life is, relative to the world that surrounds me. Indeed, this feels illusive when first contemplated, but it is worth the time and effort to get a handle on this measurement.

On the one hand, it is true, I think, that how people see us can be very distorted by their biases, their limited insight and vision, and, certainly, tainted by their own view of how they think that others "ought" to behave. All of this makes the prospect of assessing where we come out in the view of others pretty sketchy, I know.

This is compounded by the reality that I/we cannot always know with any clarity just how people really feel. This is because others around us can be secretive and, often, guarded with their genuine feelings about us.

For many reasons, people tend to "tell us what they think that we want to hear" or purposefully obfuscate their real feelings because of social or power feelings and fears.

So, this said, I still endeavor to find out the most accurate feeling of others towards me, even if the answer will be incomplete or even misleading. I get that others are reluctant to tell a truth that they, perhaps, never knew that they would have to express. Some may have even spent a lifetime knowing me but not stopped to give any thought to giving me a "score".

I accept this reality. Still, I believe that it is worth checking with close relations periodically to see how I'm doing in their eyes.

Many may argue this point and hold that there's so much uncertainty, for all of the reasons stated above, it is unlikely that the answers will be spot-on to the plus or minus.

And, yet again, I say that it is worth the effort to check other people's perceptions, acknowledging all the impediments to fully truthful answers.

And here's why this matters to me:

I know that what people may tell me is purely "feedback". It stands not for a Universal Truth, but it is possibly their individual truth and I can make some use of that.

You see, if I never ask, I just rely on "signals" imbedded in the behavior of others towards me. These signals are wildly interpretational and I will be learning very little about my impact that may be actionable.

On the other hand, I have often broken through with those close to me in order to learn their perspective of how I am coming across and how any variety to actions might improve my behavior going forward. And this does have meaning.

Besides, I sure believe that others' views can become cumulative and take on deeper meaning when the same impression is shared by multiple parties' feedback. Now, I'm getting somewhere.

So, what does this have to do with "Value"?

The Oxford Dictionary defines "Value" this way:

noun
  1.
  the regard that something is held to deserve; the importance,
      worth, or usefulness of something.
  "your support is of great value"
  synonyms: worth, usefulness, advantage, benefit, gain, profit,
      good, help, merit, helpfulness, avail; More

  2.
  a person's principles or standards of behavior; one's judgment
      of what is important in life.
  "they internalize their parents' rules and values"
  synonyms: principles, ethics, moral code, morals, standards,
      code of behavior
  "society's values are passed on to us as children"

It is a simple and quite common occurrence for all of us to tell ourselves, in all matters, what we <u>want to believe</u>. And, unchecked against the perceptions and observations of others, it is a simple matter to build a very false narrative that we repeat to ourselves over and over, as though repetition guarantees that it is true.

I, for one, do not choose to live my life this way. I do want to get an objective handle on the impact of who I am (i.e., how I behave) and how others profit or fail to profit from that way of being. It is only in approximating that imperfect sense that I can select my actions into the future – increasing, decreasing, or even revamping entirely.

And here we are at the core of my point.

My value in living in this lifetime derives, I think, entirely by my ability to impact the lives of others. To the degree that this is a positive impact, I have lived a good life. To the degree that I have had a negative impact, well, the opposite is also true.

Well, this does now get to the very purpose of my being.

I know (not just "believe", because that's too light a word) that my meaningfulness in this world is solely judged by degree and depth of my impact on others and that says a mouthful.

Yes, we are all part of a great whole – humanity. Just as in small celled organism, we are dependent on each other for survival. And, I would add, we are here to collectively support individual happiness within EVERY member of society, not just our own.

I'd go so far as to say that <u>my own happiness is critical to who I am</u>. But, my happiness is impossible unless all others surrounding and associating with me are happy, too.

Well, more on this in my next book.

What Legacy do I choose to leave behind?

This is a question that I have found myself asking more often as I have aged and I know now that I am nearer to the end of my life than to the beginning.

There are several aspects to this consideration.

First, I ask myself if how I am remembered by others really matters to me?

As a younger adult, I would have been less inclined to care about this than I am now. Maybe that is because when younger the end of my life did seem extremely far in the future and was more myth than an imminent sense of reality.

But now, as I approach my 70th birthday, I feel more determined to not only leave some form of a donation to the world (art, literature, philosophy, and the like) but also to ensure that as many others who follow are aware of my legacy, as possible.

For many others, I know that such legacies as Family, Work, Friendships, and so forth, constitute the most representative Opus of their lives. I agree wholeheartedly.

As we approach the end of our days, many of us reflect on the wonderful Family that we have developed and left behind. The Family members, we believe, represent a reflection of the values and examples that we inspired in them. And for many, this is sufficient. That makes perfect sense to me and I admire all who derive such pride, rightfully glowing at the mark on the world that their heirs represent – generation after generation.

For me, however, there's more.

I have a fervent desire to leave a great family who will feel that I made a difference in their lives in a profound way. But, I also would like to leave an imprint in the society of humans that is larger than the family gift.

I decided a while ago to leave an impact of a substantial proportion. So, I have watched, over the years, to find the topic or niche that best allows me to contribute and make a lasting difference on many.

I have now, late in life, focused on the idea that I have something to say, something to contribute to the thoughts and truths of this world in which I live. This is best summed up as: I know that, above all, people need hope to persevere and find their joyous way through life.

So, I decided on two projects to dedicate myself to that will help others on their journey.

First, I have begun a project to encourage and lift folks who are over age 60, or so, by showing the way to keep our chins up and greet each aging process in a joyful proportion.

I consider this book to be a first such attempt.

But beyond this, I am determined to start a series of local centers where seniors can get education and encouragement about the aging process and about so many options that exist to find joy and contentment.

These centers will be similar in style and set up to college-level Career Centers where classes and resources and coaching abound to point the attendee in a positive direction in their lives. I know that this is needed, but I do not believe that they exist currently.

How will this unfold? Stay tuned.

And, secondly, I am determined to help people who fear the inevitability of death to cheerfully embrace this reality. Yes, I believe that there is joy, even in the experience of death.

Towards this end, I have begun another book titled: <u>*Living Well Until the Very Last Smile*</u>.

In addition to writing this book, I have recently finished a screen play about a young doctor who dies, but is quickly reborn with his entire memory from the previous life from the moment that he opens his eyes.

Of course, the concept here is a story meant to change the narrative about life from a Western Centric View with a beginning and an end to an essentially perpetual life scenario. This latter view that we always have existed and always will, is dominant throughout Eastern religions.

The notion of eternality of existence is something that I find more probable (everything else in our world seems to reemerge after its "death" – why would we humans be the only exception?) than the Western concept.

So, by writing a play (movie, some day?) that follows a person who has died but is reborn, I am able, I hope to give some hope to those who are dying that this death is not the end, just a step through eternal life. My story gives the doctor a recovered memory that is crystal clear and allows him to tell others that it appears that death is just a crossing to a new chapter in a life.

Well, we'll see if that story line catches on. But, I'm feeling quite satisfied with the writing effort because of the positive impact for people about this very fundamental question.

I want to impact my fellow man and this is just one way to do so and, I figure, if this allows even one person to relax and feel the joy in each day, now hoping that death is NOT the end, then in yet another way, my life (this time around) will have had a deeper and tangible meaning.

These are the legacies that I am endeavoring to leave behind. I feel good about this meaning in my life.

CHAPTER 10

The FEAR of Aging

NOW WE ARE at the point of telling some hard truths to ourselves.

First, we ARE afraid. There. I said it. And you know that this is a true statement.

We are afraid of the infirmities of aging, as well as the prospect of our mortality. We are just plain afraid to die.

And, here's my bottom line in this matter: The sooner that we can just admit to these fears, the sooner we will be able to look them in the eye and start managing our way to a joyful aging process.

It's just that simple. As always, our very first challenge is to <u>admit</u> hard truths. And not only are most of us adept at avoiding seeing our truths, we live in a society that is hell bent on reinforcing all the avoidance messages that we clearly prefer.

On the one hand, as we age, we are surrounded by a retail industry whose advertising is geared solely to show elders who are spry, athletic, attractive, and always smiling, though you are never sure what they must be smiling about – the product being sold, one would assume.

And, don't get me wrong. I am a 100% advocate of smiling. I think that a smile really is the portal to the soul that both reveals what one is feeling, but also creates a condition to consistently feel better and better ("fake it 'til you make it").

The most obvious caution regarding the advertised youthful elders is that most of us are not them! And, I know that this realization, plastered before us over and over each day, can cause some to feel like a lesser person because they just can't "measure up" to the perky faces that purport to represent today's elder.

And, yes, let me note a few thoughts on the topic of "death".

Death in our culture is deeply feared and talking about the topic is to be avoided at all costs.

In short, our culture is DEEPLY afraid of death. How do we know this?

Well, our society has ceased to use the word "death", for the most part. Did you notice that, too?

For example, if your Aunt Tilley should die tonight, when someone calls you on the phone to tell you of this event they are most likely to say to you, "Hi. I thought you would want to know that Tilley <u>passed</u> tonight... or, she <u>passed on</u> ... or, she <u>passed away</u>" ... or, my personal favorite, "<u>we lost her</u>" ... or something as equally nonsensical.

This trend in our vocabulary is dangerous, I think.

These are euphemisms. They are ways of talking about something without saying the most accurate word.

This trend is dangerous because it tends to extend the fear of saying the accurate word ("died" or "dead" or "death") because it indicates, in an unsubtle way, that the event that the word is meant to describe (dying) is somehow so bad, so horrible, that we cannot speak its name. And the impact of all of this is clearly to perpetuate a fear that may not be warranted, but has become embedded in our vocabularies without consideration of the meaning of doing so.

Now, I admit that I am not the originator of this observation.

In fact, Mark Twain originally referred to this phenomenon and its negative impact when he wrote: "You can tell when a society is collectively most afraid of something. It's the moment when the entire society changes the name of that feared thing...".

Many years later, the great American Philosopher, George Carlin (also a comedian) repeated this theme to audiences demonstrating the real meaning behind the use of euphemisms and the destructive psycho-pathology of these lapses of conscience.

To me, the greatest negative impact of using these euphemisms is that our generation is passing along the fear of the real topic (death) to our succeeding generations. Yes, our children are watching us insert these silly phrases and they must assume from that observation that the topic of death must be so horrible and so necessary to be avoided because it is too painful to even name correctly. Wow. They must see this as a terrible thing (death). Why, the adults in their lives won't even utter the word. Scary, indeed.

So, I have begun talking about this phenomenon in every lecture that I deliver on the topic of aging.

I am determined to change the trajectory and the avoidance of the real word, when talking about death. To not do so, casts the notion of this most common and basic of human experiences into a light of unreal myth and symbol where we will collectively reinforce the idea that this phenomenon, death, is something other than the natural and life affirming end of a beautiful journey.

To not acknowledge and become comfortable with the idea that each of us will, indeed, die, would be like a maestro creating a beautiful concerto without a great finish – one that just stops and leaves the audience on the edge of their seats wondering if there is more or if something happened to the conductor or the sound system. Yes, the audience would just sit in their seats and watch as the orchestra disassembles their instruments and leaves the stage.

Eventually, the audience will stand and file out, but all the while they will look over their shoulders at the now empty stage thinking, "Surely there must be more".

And life would be like that, too, if it weren't for the many steps and stages of the dying process at the end of one's life, assuming one does not die in a sudden and dramatic way.

Notice, when the situations present themselves, the dramatic difference between a family's processing of a lengthy and planned death of a member vs. the chaos and drama of a sudden death, as in an auto accident.

I believe that the stages of grief that a family experiences are the same in both cases, but the stages are radically more jumbled and confused when the death was unforeseen and, hence, unprepared. Thus, the family experience is notably more dramatic and wrenching and the pain is very different in not having time to prepare and adjust.

So, how this impacts me is that, observing this difference, and appreciating the need for my family to prepare for my death (as well as for me to do so), I entered a considered plan for how my death will be orchestrated, depending on my health circumstances at the time.

To learn more about this family agreement that I called my "Care Contract", see Chapter 20. It is a document that sets the stage for my remaining years and, eventually my death by making sure that all who are and will be involved in my final years of life are on the same page. **And that page is MY page, not theirs.** It is, after all, my death – the end to my life and I fully intend for this to be a capstone event, an orchestrated exit from the stage of this life. Of course, although I intend to enjoy my life until the very end, I hope that the curtain doesn't drop, so to speak, for many years.

My goal, now, is to live to pass 100 years. Well, that's my goal, anyway. I tell everyone who listens that if I don't make it to my goal – so sue me!

Other fears about Aging

> ☐ Incapacity
> ☐ Friends and family will die before I do
> ☐ The aches and pains
> ☐ Loneliness
> ☐ Will I really have enough money to maintain a comfortable living?
> ☐ What will I do when I should stop driving? How will I know that it's time to stop?

Certainly, there are many fears that each of us has about the prospect of growing older. Here are a few of the most potent ones:

Incapacity

Throughout our lives, we have watched our elders morph from energetic and vibrant adults to frail, slow moving people who seem to look less and less like themselves physically. And, in every case, their memory has slowed considerably and some have succumbed to Alzheimer's Disease and forgotten just about everything.

There is a clear and present fear that grips all of us, to differing degrees, as we notice changes in ourselves accompanying the increase in our age.

I remember the first time that I noticed that my formerly robust and intricate memory was no longer functioning.

Since I had relied on my iron clad ability to recall anything that I had heard, for up to a year of more, the incremental loss of this ability was professionally and personally embarrassing, even if I was the only one who really noticed.

And then there were the physical abilities that became lesser and lesser. In earlier life, I had been a long-distance runner (6 to 10 miles, several times a week) and I prided myself on my ability to maintain my weight and agility, at least better than most of my family and friends.

But, as the years passed, I ran less and less. I assumed that this was because as I rose in leadership and responsibilities in organizations, I simply had less and less time for running. Eventually, it was just too painful to run, so I set schedules to work out in gyms, but that would only last for a few months at a time and, eventually, I abandoned any illusion that I would ever actually do these things again.

I accepted my growing girth as a part of the natural aging process and a sign of maturity. I started using jovial phrases for myself such as, "Pleasingly Plump" and settled into my new, larger image and stopped trying at all.

For many of us, these kinds of noticeable changes seem to sneak up on us, but we deny that they are permanent and we tell ourselves, and anyone who will listen, that this is only temporary and when the stars align, we will return to our old habits that kept us fit and youthful looking.

But, to tell the truth, there is a fear that many or most of us feel that a return to a youthful self is not really going to happen, no matter what we do or tell ourselves and others.

And, herein lies a deep and terrifying fear. This is about the time in our lives when we realize that the hour glass of time for our life and mobility is speeding along and this is very scary for most of us.

We have, so many times over the years, observed other (usually older) folks who get from place to place by wheel chair. We have, probably, deferred to them when getting onto an elevator and, deep down, we saw them as terribly unfortunate and assuaged ourselves with the belief that we would never find ourselves in such a state of immobility.

And then, we can see mobility aids in our stars. We see ourselves slowing down and know that the ability to get from place to place is not always going to be as simple as we have become used to.

So, this physical evolution is a gripping fear for most of us that are paying attention. Usually, we keep these thoughts to ourselves, or share these with only a few close confidants.

Sufficiently alarmed? I'll address some thoughts for how to manage our way through this fear in the next chapter.

Friends and family will die before I do

This is a very common concern that I hear quite often from my over-60 friends.

As we age, we see the friends and relatives of others in terrible grief over the loss of life time friends and relations. We often feel helpless to console others and part of the helplessness is spurred by the realization that this acute sense of loss may well come our way, too.

And this is one of those deep-seated realities from which there is no escape, the older we get.

And, in fact, these losses bring into focus a related fear – our own mortality. Yes, it is easy to sublimate any thoughts of our own death amidst the day to day activities and commerce of life. But, then someone very close to us falls ill and dies and the inevitability of our own death comes front and center in our minds, even causing occasional loss of sleep and general distress.

I have been experiencing this repeated loss cycle in my own life and I can attest to its power and fear.

As the saying goes, we get past each of these losses and pick ourselves up and go forward with a measure of sadness that wasn't there before and a permanent feeling of missing first this person, then another.

In a few pages, I will share some thoughts about these losses that have been helpful to me over the years. Please look for these in the next chapter.

The aches and pains

Well here is one of the most common fears that people have shared with me. This is the fear of all the aching and painful joints and other bodily parts that seems to be the case universally as our peers and seniors have aged.

Now, I admit that this is a realistic fear that is about the natural design of our body parts that have served us so well in our youth – the ability to run and jump and contort as needed through our teen years and twenties.

And then, somewhere in our mid to late thirties, we start realizing that body parts are no longer as flexible as we had become accustomed and even consistent exercise programs are more and more challenging.

And even if we resist the temptation to complain to others, all of us, I believe, harbor a fear that we will certainly have some number of years of life where we will suffer bodily degradation and that this suffering will absorb the second half of the years of our life. And, although many of my peers have sown played this fear, I know that it is there and the fear alone will make our journey into our second half of life a more dramatic and sad experience than we would wish.

I have passed through the stages of aging where this fear has raised its head. I have now moved into the actual age range where these pains have taken center stage. So, let me share some thoughts in the next chapter about how else to look at this phenomenon.

Loneliness

Here is a fear that has popped up for many of us at various times throughout our lives.

While we were younger and working, we had naturally occurring social situations (people at work, family, and so forth) that were at least able to abate these feelings. Still, the fear of becoming lonely has nagged at many throughout their lives.

But the fear of this kind of heavy burden as a part of the reality of old age, has weighed on many and caused a deep and genuine dread of the onset of one's later years. It feels to many as if this loneliness is "cooked into" the years that lay ahead due to the likelihood that others in our family and friends will die or become too ill to socialize leaving us to a lonely existence. Hopeless and alone.

If this is a fear of yours, please read my thoughts on this topic in the next chapter. You will read about how I have approached this fear and found a way to manage it.

Will I really have enough money to maintain a comfortable living?

No matter how much we have saved, and planned, and put into motion a smart investment program, I believe that every one of us new retirees (and older ones) asks these questions of ourselves – have I done enough? Will something unforeseeable arise that will deplete my savings, just when I must rely on them the most? And, might something change in the national economy or federal programs that will negatively impact my nest egg?

I will admit that these questions are there for me, too. Especially when I witness the great uncertainties in the Congress that give me pause. I mean, I can easily see where certain forces within the federal legislature will deem it popular to pander to ultra conservative ideologies by drastically reducing the effectiveness of the retirement related financial programs. After all, it seems that more and more financially wealthy folks are running for and being elected to the Congress. I don't believe that these folks are inclined to take the needs of the average Joe (me and you?) into account as they slice and dice social programs for the sake of cost savings.

Add to this the reality that prices are always increasing while our personal health is less likely to allow us to return to work over the years.

So, yes. The concern is there for most of us that our cash and savings may not stretch as far as they will need to for our retirement to be comfortable and worry free.

But, even here, I have found peace of mind and a way to keep this in perspective to enjoy each day with only minimal worry. I'll share that set of thoughts in the next chapter. Stay tuned.

What will I do when I should stop driving? How will I know that it's time to stop? How will I get around thereafter?

So, have you had the difficult occasion to request that an elder stop driving and turn over their car keys because it's become too unsafe? Oh, that is a VERY special experience – one that I do not wish to repeat.

The problem is that this conversation is ALWAYS a thorny and embarrassing one. The elder is seldom prepared to hear this request and they will argue the point for all that they are worth.

And, you know why this will be the case, don't you? In a word: Freedom. Yes, driving for so many of us (if not most) represents the freedom to come and go as we need and see fit. It represents a level of freedom that eclipses the riding of public transportation or the offer of a ride from others. In those cases, we are limited to the schedules of the public conveyance or that of another driver. And, once we have tasted the freedom to move about on our own schedule and at our own pace, reverting to the alternatives is just irksome, to say the least.

And, there it is in a nutshell. No one wants to give up the freedom to leave any location when they please and get themselves to the next location on their own schedule.

Thus, a person who should not continue driving will demonstrate extraordinary denial and want deeply to believe that their skills on the road are just fine, despite overwhelming evidence to the contrary. This leads to an ugly confrontation when even a close loved one introduces the subject of the elder's driving abilities and leads to typically awful scenes where statements are made by both sides that, usually, far exaggerate the observable realities – in both directions.

And yet, inevitably, if an elder is lucky enough to live long enough, the day will come when their skill at driving will give way to their diminished senses.

And here's the irony. You, the reader, and I, the writer, can easily see how diminished senses and cognition will arrive with age and, to be sure, impact our own ability to drive an automobile safely. We know that. It's just as sure as can be. And, yet, won't we be just like all who have gone before us? Won't we, predictably, be incapable of objectivity as our safe driving abilities wane? And, hence, won't we fuss and deny when confronted by others who threaten to remove this privilege of a lifetime?

In the next chapter, I will share with you the actions that I used to manage this reality for me. I can't guarantee that these steps will work for all. But, I am confident that they made a lot of sense. And, when the time came, it worked without the ugly family angst that we (my family and I) would have experienced without the plan that I enacted. Read that chapter and, perhaps, learn of at least one way of managing this coming difficulty.

CHAPTER 11

The REALITY of Aging

- ☐ Incapacity
- ☐ Friends and family will die before I do
- ☐ The aches and pains
- ☐ Loneliness
- ☐ Will I really have enough money to maintain a comfortable living?
- ☐ What will I do when I should stop driving? How will I know that it's time to stop?

Incapacity and the aches and pains

While I recognize that the fear of being incapacitated is very real and not to be minimized, I have decided to face my own fear head on.

I fully recognize that the processes of both bodily and mental decline have begun in earnest. I am just now turning seventy and I am surprised daily when I realize that I have somehow made it to this age. In truth, inside I feel like I'm still in my thirties – at least in terms of the wonderment of each day and how I am still looking forward to so much more life. And, that is not a fabricated feeling. It is genuine.

So, here's how I get there.

First, I am determined to live authentically. I do not wish to deny things that I and others can observe to be happening. But, rather, I want to own that my reality is just that – real. I find myself mentioning how I'm doing with truth, but without exaggeration. So, when another asks me how I am doing, I assume that they really want to know and I tell them.

I speak of my changes with a smile on my face, always. This is because I know that what I am experiencing is real but also just as natural as can be. Yes, I keep reminding myself that the way my body now behaves (within the limitations of decline) is the way that it was designed to operate. I do not for a minute believe that this is any form of retribution or plain bad luck.

No, my bodily and mental capacities are natural and they form an important part of my new reality. That is the reality of a 70-year-old guy who carries too much weight but is also the product of a family whose members of both sexes live minimally into their late 80's and many to late 90's. (I'm determined to be the first to make it 100!)

And here's the real key: I believe that each of us has a choice in how we react to the decline of our physical and mental abilities. Our choice is to either see the aches and pains and mental slow-down as a horrible curse that invites extreme unhappiness – OR – we can see the changes as simply a fact of life for those lucky enough to have lived to an older age.

I should add that I have further determined to see all changes with a rich sense of humor. Yes, I laugh out loud every day of my life now – mostly at the limitations of my body and mind.

I am, by choice, paying attention to the many new (mostly small) aches and pains, the noises that my bones now make as I walk, and, of course, the things that my body part now seem to have their own mind about – they just don't work the way that they used to, or when they used to. And, most comical of all, there are body parts that work when they aren't supposed to. And all of this just makes me laugh.

Well, in addition to laughing, I also spend thoughtful time designing ways to manage the operations of my body parts. It takes a bit of research and thought but, when I can set aside any judgements or labels about what I experience, I can design how to remain comfortable even if the systems seem to all go haywire at once (every now and then).

In sum, I just don't allow any time to feel sorry for myself or to complain. After all, these are the natural things that come with aging and the good news is: I made it this far! I am delighted to be able to say (write) this.

Finally, I avoid the temptation to define myself by any of my malfunctions. I have noticed that many others fall into this trap, but I refuse to join them.

The doctors have told me that in the next few years that I will require walking assistance – a can, then a walker, and then a wheelchair. I am determined that when these things occur, I will tell jokes about them and, above all, I will appreciate that the device allows me to continue to get around and that's to be cherished!

Friends and family will die before I do

This is a universal concern, isn't it?

And, this phenomenon has already started for me. I went through the early life losses of a friend in High School who died in an automobile crash. Also, my very best friend in the Marine Corps died in a helicopter crash when we were in our early 20s.

And then there were the middle life losses of my parents, grandparents, and so many Aunts and Uncles.

I can share that these earlier deaths were certainly difficult and caused long periods of grieving for me. But in those instances, I was surrounded by family and friends – all of us going through the stages of grief together and finding ways to support one another.

So, now I have passed through my 60's, beginning my 70's and a new set of losses has begun.

One of my oldest and dearest friends died suddenly of a heart attack last year. Even though I was aware that he was not well, it came as a shock to get the call. Reality now sets in and I think about my remaining friends as being as fragile as I am and this reminds me of our certain mortality.

But, here's the thing.

I know that it is impossible that all of my remaining family and friends will simply live as long as I do. Either I will die and leave them all to grieve or they will die and I will grieve. There is no third choice.

So, this is simply a reality of the aging experience. Although it is not a notion that I dwell upon, I do recognize that this is the deal. And, there is one bright opportunity.

This realization can cause us to soberly acknowledge a reality that <u>our relationships are just for a time</u>.

The choice is to either ruminate and feel badly about this reality, OR we can **decide** to enjoy every day and every moment of every encounter that remains with loved ones.

We can also decide to live so that we will die with no regrets. This is not easy to do, but I have decided to manage all of my relationships with a loving soul – speaking the truth to all, living authentically, and, above all, making room in my heart to ask for forgiveness where needed, and to offer forgiveness to all.

Plus, the experience of the death of someone so close to me for most of my life has caused me to reconsider the small annoyances of my life and, well, just to slow down and rapidly dismiss the trivial as being unworthy of a spike in my blood pressure. I'm sure that even small anger slices off time from my life and that's just not worth it.

This is the path of my life's journey now. I offer this to you as food for thought.

Loneliness

The fear that for a variety of reasons we may end up living alone and be lost in a feeling of loneliness is very common. I have heard this fear expressed by a wide variety of folks over the years and it has made me wonder why I have not thought of, much less dwelled on, this potential for myself.

As I think about this phenomenon and danger, a couple of insights have presented themselves as germane to explain my lack of concern here.

First, I realize that there is a huge difference between a reality of being *"alone"*, by one's self in any circumstance, and a feeling of *"loneliness"*. The first describes a state of existing where one is not surrounded by others for long swaths of time. The second is a *feeling* that many have described to me, but that I cannot recall ever having felt at any point in my life. That feeling is a level of sadness that arises from inside oneself in reaction to the realization that no one else is near.

I think that this chart explains the social need differences among people.

Social Needs Spectrum

Cannot be Alone   Either Way   Hermit
PRIMARY SOCIAL   **LONE WOLF**

As you can see in the spectrum above, I believe that a small percentage of people (maybe 5 to 10 percent) are unable to cope with being by themselves for any appreciable period. When left alone, they become anxious and in need of finding others with whom to share the time.

Then there are high percentage (about 25% according to Isabel Myers of the Myers – Briggs Organization) who don't have a need to have others around. In fact, the extreme of this group, what I call the "hermits", prefer to be by themselves and would have it that way always, if that is possible. People on this end of the spectrum are commonly called, "Introverts".

But many people (the remaining 75 percent, or so) are just fine and can enjoy their time and circumstances whether on their own or with others.

This is just a difference in people – some are susceptible to a feeling arising out of being by themselves, even for a short duration. Indeed, I have known very rational and self-aware folks who have a deep-seated need to have others around them at any given time, even if they are not exchanging conversation. I do not choose to judge people who feel this way. They are certainly entitled to feel this way, and, indeed, they are far from being in the minority in society.

I imagine that there is something primal about this phenomenon that harkens back to early man who was only "safe" when others of their species were nearby. This would seem to equate to an assumption that there is safety in numbers and that the individual is far less likely to be attacked or harmed when others are near.

I would grant to this is a real and natural feeling. It seems to explain the related need that some of these very same people must be in the company of other animals who provide companionship and, at a primal level, perhaps, safety (there is a mutual pact to protect each other should the need arise).

And then there are people like me. We are not in any way superior to the others. We are just plain different. I am describing people like myself for whom the desire has never arisen to be in the company of others (not even "pets") to feel comfortable and well entertained. Yes, we are the folks who are just fine when others are around, but when left to our own devices, we are at ease and find ways to manage our time without a thought about "missing" the company of others, until others are present. In other words, we are just fine either way.

What I am describing for myself and others is a middle ground between those who are in constant need of the presence of others and those who prefer the life of a hermit.

We, in the middle ground, are just fine with others around or when by ourselves, even for days at a time.

I would assume that therefore a person like me doesn't worry that old age will be a lonely time. We have always been able to get along just fine when surrounded by others or on our own.

And, besides, I have known folks who tell me that they can be in a crowded room and yet feel lonely. This, I presume, is due to a feeling of connectivity to those around, or lack thereof.

In any event, I do believe that when planning the future for ourselves, we should strongly consider which of the social types we are (needing others around to avoid feeling lonely, just fine on our own, or a true hermit who prefers a singular life) to appropriately design the late life arrangements to be made.

Will I really have enough money to maintain a comfortable living?

Until you read this book, you may have thought that this is the only real worry that people who Retire will have. But, indeed, this is a realistic concern.

The most fear of this topic arises out of the fact that we cannot know what we don't know.

We have, no doubt, planned our savings and investments over the years and our arithmetic tells us that there should be enough to live comfortably, in financial terms.

But what we don't know is how damaging unexpected events will impact us. For example, will our family seniors run into financial difficulties and need to rely on us for support? This can represent a large unplanned expense.

Also, will our children run into financial difficulties and we may want to help them, as always? This happens and can even result in a perceived need to allow them to move back in with no income to add to the household budget. This turn of events is at once dramatic and, potentially, devastating.

And, how about changes in federal laws that directly impact our nest egg? Tax laws can change. Social Security is constantly a topic of threat by our lawmakers. And various other income and securities can change such as a stock market swing.

So, I'm describing several unknown but possible scenarios that can alter our plans and financial picture.

But I would point out that these possibilities are the normal risks of living. My own plan is to keep my eye on the global and national landscape to watch for changes that may impact me. I must then adjust accordingly.

As for the increased financial responsibilities of taking on elder or child care, I plan to be judicious and follow these steps:

1. Understand the problem that presents itself fully and seek professional counsel to see solutions

2. Enlist family and friends as resources to either brainstorm or collaborate to find solutions along the way

3. Be honest with myself about my ability to take on the financial needs of others when there is a social community network of assistance that can be researched and tapped for help

4. Recognize that all throughout my life there have been uncertainties and both minor and major events that have tested my planning and personal resources. But, the fact is that I have come through all of those and eventually landed on my feet.

I have confidence that I will be adaptive as I enjoy my Retirement years for as long as my intellect allows.

What will I do when it's time to stop driving? How will I know that it's time to stop?

In chapter 20 of this book, I share an idea about an agreement between myself and my family in which I call my *Care Contract*. I will describe in that chapter all the decisions that I have formulated and shared with my family. I insisted that they sign the document to acknowledge that they know and understand that these instructions are my desires for how my later life is to unfold, dependent only on the changes in my health.

I dedicated a section of that agreement to my wishes for when I should stop driving and how to implement the disposal of my car. You will see the details in Chapter 20 but I'll make the case for my choices here.

First, I believe quite strongly that I am a thinking and feeling person. Thus, I don't need to rely on cliché's or any standard other than reason. Also, I believe that this is a topic of such immense importance during my life that I decided to research the topic and think it through while I was in my early 60's – while I was still compos mentis enough to think clearly.

So, here's how I proceeded.

I recognized, first, that one of my core values is the preservation of life and the personal duty to create no harm to any other person. This is fundamental to who I am and I feel that decisions such as the cessation of any dangerous activity should be guided by this value.

Next, I told myself a truth. If I am lucky, I will live to an age where either physical or mental changes will affect the safety of my driving abilities. This happens to everyone who reaches their 80's and 90's and I intend to be in that club. Thus, there will surely come a time when I will no longer be able to drive with the level of safety for myself and others that reason demands.

So, I wrote an instruction to my family, telling them the above thoughts and I provided them with a list of actions that would certainly demonstrate that my driving abilities have degraded to a point of unsafety.

I didn't pull this list out of thin air. I lifted a listing of driver behaviors from the web site of the National Transportation Safety Board and inserted it onto the page of my contract. This is a well-researched list of the most common behaviors of older drivers that indicate that they are past their driving days.

In my contract, I have instructed my family to inform me of my entry into a driving prohibitive stage, and, in fact, how to ask me for my car keys and then dispose of my car. Please see this topic in Chapter 20. I am sure that you will be entertained and, hopefully, you will find the motivation to follow suit.

And, now, there is one more item to describe: **What to do, once we're no longer driving**.

PART FOUR

Decisions Regarding
Retirement Fully
Preparing Ourselves
Emotionally And
Socially (Beyond
Financial Planning)

We can retire from a job, but we can never retire from Life.
Daisaku Ikeda
21st Century Japanese Poet and Philosopher

CHAPTER 12

What is "Retirement"?

IN THIS CHAPTER, I would like to get us all onto the same page about how to define: Retirement after which we'll look at some of the common fears about the prospect of retiring and, well, aging in general.

So, first, let's define Retirement.

When I ask my audiences to tell what they first think of when they hear the word, "Retirement", I repeatedly hear such phrases as:

- **It's Freedom**
- **Relaxation**
- **My time is my own**
- **SLEEP!**
- **Travel**
- **Time with Family**
- **Catch up on LIFE**

And, so forth.

Well, I can't disagree with any of those thoughts because Retirement offers all those opportunities, and many more.

I would like to add some thoughts to this mix, though, that I think may be helpful.

Here goes:

WHAT IS RETIREMENT?

The concept: This is a transition "to" not "from" life – to actively pursue goals determined by <u>Who We Are</u> – no coincidences – **We can re-invent ourselves**!

Yes, that's it. The best word that I can think of to describe the phenomenon of Retirement decision making: **Reinvention**.

So many people who, upon Retirement claiming to have found fulfillment, have reported that they decided to set aside the images of their work roles and imagine themselves doing something with most of their Retired time that promised pleasure and allowed them a new identity.

Now the idea of "Identity" is crucial. Here's why.

Particularly here in the United States, many of us (if not all) find our self-identity in large part by way of the work that we do. Seems true, doesn't it? Have you noticed how people who are meeting us for the first time ask us what we do, before they ask about most anything else?

And, we are comforted to be able to deliver an answer that describes us favorably, such as, "Oh, I'm a Physician", or "a Grocer", or "a Legal Assistant". These statements about our jobs are only descriptive of the job that we hold, but the title of the job also contains a societal level of esteem that provides a built-in self-flattery or, perhaps, an embarrassment.

In fact, our culture has this automatic mechanism built in that feeds our self-image, both positively and negatively. We have been taught since childhood about the reverence or disdain that will be associated with different career choices. These set in early and stick for a lifetime.

Thus, we allow ourselves to feel good in our self-concept if we are doing (working at) a profession of any sort and to the degree that Society teaches us to value that job and its title.

And, herein lies a fault line. Since the above described connection of job and ego (self-image) represents a very strong hold on our concept of ourselves, imagine the disconnect that a person feels at the very instant that they learn that they are no longer employed.

I have been witness to this gut-wrenching realization at least a thousand times during the years that I counseled people in the immediate aftermath of job loss ("Down-sizing",

"Lay-Off", "Firing", or the like). I learned that the deep fear and feelings of desperation were universal, shop workers to CEOs alike. Of course, I recall the same discomfort at times when I left jobs, too.

What's interesting to report is that the deadly fear that churned in my innards at these moments were as much present when I had chosen to leave a job, as when the leaving was chosen for me – with or without notice. Has this happened to you or to anyone that you know? I'll bet that you've seen this happen, as well.

Now consider the inevitable "Retirement" event for so many of us.

This is supposed to be a time when we are skipping in the streets, laughing at all our neighbors who still are leaving for their jobs while we will spend our days in care-free enjoyment doing whatever suits us from moment to moment.

But, wait. So often, recent Retirees are anything but joyful. In fact, they are often confused about how to use the many hours of each day that are no longer being devoted to work. And, there are days (and nights) when these recently liberated professionals cower in fear of the unknown and feeling that they no longer readily possess an "Identity" – not like they were used to enjoying, anyway.

Here are some starting thoughts:

The <u>fuel</u> for a happy Retirement is this: **Live with a PURPOSE!** Every day – **<u>have a plan</u>** and **<u>Create Value</u>**

Here's what I mean.

First, a sense of **Purpose** is, I believe, an integral part of the fabric of who we (you and me) are. **Purpose** has been cooked into every job that we have held, no matter it's level of activity or consequence.

I know how it has felt for me when, at the end of most every day, I have been able to return home and feel, at least subconsciously, that "I mattered today... It made a difference that I was there, today... What I, and/or my team, is doing really matters."

What a great feeling that has been! Sure, the money that I have been paid to do every job that I have held has been important to me. But, in the end, the finest and most satisfying "payoff" for doing the work that I have had the privilege to perform, has been the feeling of satisfaction that my efforts meant something – to somebody.

And, <u>herein lies a danger</u>, once Retired or in any way out of work.

The sense of **Purpose** that we have enjoyed, even unconsciously, for so the years of our working life has formed a large part of our identity. In a very real way, it has helped to express who we are. It has comforted us when work was challenging and we have felt the admiration of others within our closest associations where our over-all feeling of self-worth has resided.

Then, one day, post-Retirement or any work cessation (laid-off, down-sized, restructured, or any cause of action that resulted in our being out of work) we find ourselves, often sub-consciously, fighting to find a return to feeling good about ourselves.

And the reason that we are often least likely to identify for our feeling of lowered self-worth, is the lack of a **Purpose** in our life, at that juncture.

This has been shown to me by several Retirees who feel lost, listless, depressed, and, perhaps, rudderless.

I had a neighbor when I lived at Leisure World, a Retirement village outside of Washington, DC, who told me once that he had sunk into a deep depression because he could not put his finger on a REASON to even get himself out of bed each day. His life since Retirement had revolved around his wife. He was her care giver when she became terminally ill. He kept her at home, at her request, and saw to her every need.

This went on for over three years. During this time, he felt sad to be losing the love of his life, but he had a reason to live and to accomplish things every day to keep her comfortable and loved for the balance of her life.

Then, in the months after her death, he fell into a deep depression. In addition to the loss of his partner, he realized that he had not discovered another "project" or aim to focus his attention on. He could not describe a **Purpose** for his life. He was sad. He was inconsolable.

But as I got to know him and encouraged him to share his talents and interests, he began to make lists. These were lists of activities that he might do that would again awaken a sense of being needed.

I am a great believer in the value of Service – Volunteering, that is. Giving ourselves to others in terms of our talents and time, releases a new sense of **Purpose** that propels our life. This is what I would refer to as: **Creating Value**.

I have found it incredibly valuable to make a list of what things I want to accomplish – every day, every week, and even every month. This has served me well to keep myself centered on taking action about the things that I will want to do at each of these junctures.

This has kept me more focused and able to feel a sense of accomplishment as I check things off of my list.

Of course, I never lose sight of the fact that I am retired. So, I am perfectly OK when I don't get everything done on any list. Accomplishing to do lists was important when I was working, but not so much now.

One thing that I am very glad to report is that by aligning the actions that I put on my lists with what I value, I have maintained a sense of **purpose** for things large and small. Also, by infusing within my activities things that help others and make their lives better, I feel a real sense of both accomplishment and meaning. I know that I am **creating value** for others every day.

To be specific, when I lived at a Senior Village a couple of years ago, I found a local Veterans Center where I arranged to go at least once a week to meet with fellow Veterans and coach them about how to write a resume and conducted mock interviews with them as practice to feel more comfortable in the real thing.

Why Veterans? They are my "tribe" and I had spent a thirty-four-year career as a professional in Human Resources. So, I was giving back what had made a successful career for me to a group that I care about and have real affinity for. And, in all, I was only devoting a fraction of my time (a day a week) and I was the recipient of the gratitude of those who have also served our country, while feeling, once again, that I was really making a difference in people's lives.

These are precious things indeed.

CHAPTER 13

The FEAR of Retirement and Aging

I CANNOT EMPHASIZE the following points too strongly:

Retirement is a **beginning** of something new, not just an ending.

Certainly, people often identify the idea of Retirement as the end of their working life, and this is certainly the case, unless, of course, we just take Retirement from one job and go out and start another one. This does happen, but if we start another job, at least if it's a full-time job, after "Retiring" from our current job, then we really haven't Retired yet. We have just changed jobs and that's not uncommon.

But let me talk about a true "Retirement" where we cease to work full time and enter the new world of leisure and self-directed engagement. This is the world of Retirement that most of us long for, if we have a safety net of financial and activity support.

Oh, and here's a reality that you may have already been hearing about. In general, people who retire today will live many more Retired years than those who Retired before us.

Yes, we are living longer and healthier and this is a wonderful reality. It is also a paradigm shift.

I'll let you in on an observation that I have been making of late. This is completely anecdotal, of course. I have been meeting more and more Retirees who tell me that they have been officially Retired LONGER than they worked in life. I think that this is wonderful and allows us the luxury to explore alternative ways of living for many more years. (This is now one of my Life Goals to meet or exceed.)

And, yet, sadly, I have met many older employed workers who are delaying their Retirement decision, not because of money (though that's some) but because they are afraid to start this chapter of their life.

Now here comes the fear:

I have been told by folks that they will not begin their Retirement because it is, "The beginning of the End of life." I understand that a person can feel this way and I certainly do not blame them for finding fear in this thought.

Others have told me that they are just plain afraid because they do not have a clue about what they will do with their time, once retired from work life.

Well, first, let's review the fear of the end of Life.

What about "the end"? Let me share some thoughts about this and see if it helps others tempted to draw the same conclusion as those described above.

The End

When I refer to "The End", I am indicating the end of life, known by its old-fashioned name: Death.

I have given this considerable thought.

I will join such luminaries who proceeded me as Mark Twain (Samuel Clemens) and the great American philosopher, George Carlin, as I point out the following.

Of course, there is an "end" coming for each of us. And yet we play games with our thoughts and actions about this, probably for very understandable reasons of a desire for self-preservation.

And, yet, in truth, somewhere inside we really do know that death is an inescapable reality. It's our universal destiny. Not a one of us will escape this fate. Not a one.

So, you won't be surprised to learn that I (probably like you, too, at some point) deluded myself into the bliss of ignorance about my mortality. Yes, I know this by some of the clear signals of a state of mortality-denial.

I lived into my early 60's without writing a *Last Will and Testament*. If I thought about it at all, I just shrugged and thought, "Oh, there's plenty of time to take care of that. That's a requirement for older folks. I'll certainly get to that in just a few years…" But, I didn't get to it until I was told that open heart surgery would be necessary in the next few days to fix my aortic valve, or I would surely die.

Wow! What a shock! And, what a wakeup call. Only then did I realize that I had a lot of thinking, deciding, and plain old work to do to be ready for the end of my life. Writing my Will was just the start as I also had to make decisions about how I wanted my end of life experience and what should be done about that and by whom. Well, more about that later in this book.

I want to point out here, though, that we should not be too critical of our fears about our death. We're products of our society. A society that clearly fears death in the worst way.

How do I know that society fears death? As first remarked by Mark Twain and, later, by George Carlin: "You can tell when a society really fears something. They change the language about it."

And, boy, isn't that true about death? Why in our society we no longer use the word – death, right?

If your aunt Tilly dies tonight, someone is likely to call you to let you know. But, they won't say it, will they? No. They'll get you on the phone and say, "Hi. I thought that you would want to know that Tilly *PASSED* tonight. Like, she had GAS which was the most popular original meaning of the phrase, *She Passed*. Or, they may say, "Hi, I'm sorry to be the one to tell you that *we LOST* Tilley this evening." (If she was extremely old and bed ridden, aren't you tempted to say, *"You LOST her??? Well, I'll gather a posse and we'll come over and help to find her... She's pretty slow. She couldn't have gotten far!"*

Yes, I used that response not too long ago. And, the caller quickly said, "Oh, no. I mean that she *Passed*." I said, "*Gas?*" And, exasperated, she finally said, "No, No, No, *Tilley DIED*". And, I was quick to say, well, why didn't you just <u>say so?</u>

That's how silly it has gotten. When I persisted with the caller, she blurted out, "I was just trying to be polite!"

Wow! I wondered then, and now, just when did it become *impolite* to die? When did that happen?

Well, I'm just trying to make the point that there is a societal fear of this most natural of events. And we all collude in perpetuating this fear behavior of changing the language to avoid saying, death.

But, that's a problem, I think. We have built a cascade of fears about this universal phenomenon. And it gets worse.

I see that we are passing this fear down to those who follow us.

Our succeeding generations are adopting the fear and awe of this natural turn of events because we, the seniors, are so "hinky" about it. Yes. At least subconsciously, younger folks cannot help but think that this death thing must be something very, very terrible. Sure. Why they can't help but notice that we adults won't ever SAY THE WORD. How bad must that be, they must ask?

I am taking a stand, though. I am asking readers and audiences to think about this and try to turn this back around to where death is seen as a natural event. It is the culmination of LIVING, not it's opposite, as such.

So much of the fear, of course, is anchored in the fact that at death we move from the known (life) to the unknown (not life). For this, fear is cooked in. I get that. But that doesn't have to be the end of the story.

I was very fortunate in my life to have an intellectual mentor that too few others have had.

I was raised by my maternal grandfather. He used to describe himself as "an old country doctor". He was a very practical and down-to-earth gentleman who called things in life exactly as he saw them. He did not mince words and, above all, he detested euphemisms.

He was a man who used the most precise word possible and he didn't care much about the conventions of the day. In fact, he used to tell me that the use of euphemisms was just plain "cowardice". Well, let me add, as an aside, that this conviction of his to always use plain language led to some very entertaining Sunday dinners as his wife, my grandmother, did not see this point the same way.

So, he was the first influence in my life to avoid all the other phrases and insist on words like "death" to describe the end of a person's (or a pet's) life.

And when I asked him about the meaning of death for a human, he was a font of thought-provoking ideas.

He explained to me that, as the family doctor, he was with people from their moment of birth, in so many cases, until, sometimes, their death. He had seen the full cycle, he said.

And he concluded that Birth and Death are both just parts of the cycle of Life and they are not to be feared, but enjoyed (outside of the incidence of pain).

He told me that he insisted that his patients who were truly and irrevocably in the last days and hours of their lives be discharged from the hospital. He was fully able to set them up in their home and teach the family how to care for the loved one in their final hours.

He took this very seriously. He even insisted that young children NOT be shielded from the last days of a loved one's life. But, rather children should be brought into the room and given a task to contribute to the comfort and sense of love that the dying so desperately needed to feel.

Likewise, he told me that this act of family support was a way to teach all family members that the death was not something to be feared. "It is as natural as can be", he explained. Death is inexorably a part of Life and, if possible, the dying family member should stay incorporated within the fabric of the family experience.

What wonderful life lessons I learned from him. But he wasn't done until the day of his own death.

When I was in my early 40's, he was retired and living in Florida. He called me to let me know that he had inoperable pancreatic cancer that had metastasized.

I went to visit with him while he was still in the hospital and, later, when he was at his home in hospice care.

One afternoon, I was visiting and sitting with him in his bedroom. Other family members and his hospice team who had been sitting vigil at his bedside went out for some shopping and I was alone with him for several hours.

Although he was asleep most of the time that afternoon, he awoke for a while and looked around the room. Seeing me, he smiled and beckoned me to sit on the bed next to him.

Even though his voice was very low, I could hear him clearly.

He first asked where the other family members were. I told him they went out for a bite to eat and would return soon. He was pleased that they were taking care of themselves.

He then beckoned me to come to the bed and sit beside him. When I did, he said, "Mike, why does everyone look so sad? Even you?" I said, "Pop, they tell us you are going to die." He grinned slyly and blurted out, "Michael, I am a doctor. I KNOW that I'm going to die. I have always known that." And his smile continued.

Of course, I told him that we were sad to lose him from our lives. He smiled and said, "That's not possible. I will always be with you in some way."

I told him that the doctors had briefed the family that morning that he would perhaps live a few more days or weeks. Pop said, "Oh, those silly doctors! I looked at my chart this morning when no one was looking. The doctors are just being cowardly and not telling you the truth. With my vital signs reading what they are, I'll be lucky to make it through until dawn of tomorrow."

It turned out, he was correct.

But what's most memorable to me was what he said to me in the next few moments. He said that at that exact moment in his life, he could confidently say that he was about to die – **with no regrets**.

He then encouraged me to do the same. He said that I may have many years ahead of me. Plenty of time to make mistakes, but to correct the correctable. He told me to try throughout my life to settle all things that need to be settled, as I go along.

He further encouraged me to be quick to forgive, and unafraid to ask for forgiveness.

What a great formula he gave to me to live a full life and to die with no regrets. I became fully committed to this type of life from that afternoon on. I had not previously given much thought to my death but I have since chosen to see my death as a completion of my life, well this one, anyway.

I have spent many years now enjoying each day and each person in my life as fully and as consciously as I can. I am determined to follow in my grandfather's footsteps and, above all, cease to fear the arrival of my moment of death. I see that it is just natural as part of living as can be.

In fact, I see now that it's just unlikely that death is itself an end, as such. It must also be a beginning of something – another journey.

Sure. How can it be that all things in Nature seem to die, but then return, often as something else (example: flowers and plants that die seem to always reappear even if only as fodder for the birth and growth of something else).

Why would humans be the only exception to that phenomenon? What arrogance to hold that we are so different from the balance of Nature. No, I don't buy it.

But, then, this is the stuff of great arguments. Since no one has returned to tell us any differently, we will all continue to fantasize about what comes next and build myths that make us feel more secure, and that's perfectly natural.

The fear of Retirement attached to uncertainty about what to do once Retired is quite common but also quite manageable.

We will need to answer a couple of questions for ourselves, as we ponder and stand up to this fear.

In the end, we will want to explore Who Will I Be in Retirement? As well as, what kind of socialization will allow me to be the most happy?

Who Will I Be?

This is a question that I have heard from clients over the years as they ponder the world of possible activities during Retirement. Some have said to me, "I don't know what to choose to do because I am not sure who I will be as a Retiree."

Well, my quick answer has always been: "We are the SAME person on the day <u>after</u> Retirement as the day <u>before</u> Retirement". But there's more.

There is surely a value in asking the "Who Am I?" question, the answer to which will be very helpful in making selections of activities during Retirement.

To make this point, let me address two personality measures that, knowing the answers for ourselves, will inform choices with which we will be more "ourselves" than to choose others.

First: **Dominant Behavioral Traits**

There are four primary ways of behaving that adults utilize within any social organization. A "social organization" is any group where we are surrounded by people, for example: our Family is a Social Organization and our workplace is a Social Organization (we are surrounded by people and must interact in both).

As you consider from these four basic styles to determine which one represents your preferred style, remember this: each of us has all four of these styles within us as potentials. That is, each of us can operate by way of any of the styles based on circumstances and needs in a moment.

But one of the styles, for each of us, is our most natural and desirable style in which we would prefer to operate if the circumstance allows us to. This style is our most comfortable zone of behavior. This is referred to as our Dominant Style.

I will take some time now to describe each of the four behavioral styles. You will be like most people if you recognize yourself in one of the described styles. But, don't be concerned if your Dominant Style is not obvious to you, or you feel conflicted between two, saying to yourself that you know that one of the descriptions captures your behavior, but then a second one seems likely, too.

No worries, though. After the explanations, I will give you a way to surely determine which is your Dominant Style within the four primary styles that I will now describe.

Dominant Behavioral Styles
LEFT BRAIN   RIGHT BRAIN

CLOSURE

- Logical
- Analytical
- Fact Based
- Quantitative

OPTIONS

- Intuitive
- Holistic
- Integrating
- "Outside the Box"

DETAILED

- Sequential
- Organized
- Detail Junkie
- Planner

SOCIAL

- Feelings Based
- Enthusiastic
- Thinks of Others
- Ambiguity=OK

Here's the explanation of each of these Behavior Styles. Please hang on through the explanations. See if you can see yourself in one of them and after we're done, I'll explain how knowing this about ourselves serves us in Retirement.

First, the easiest one for me to describe to you is the **SOCIAL** style. That is because this is clearly my style. I am off the scale as a **social** by all measures, so here goes.

We **Socials**, well, we just plain LIKE PEOPLE. We always have.

Social people often go into people-facing professions like Human Resources, Social Work, Sales, and so forth.

And, you have always been surrounded by **Socials** in your workplace. Here's how you have always been able to pick us out.

We are the co-workers who, when you came into our office or cubicle during the work day, always greeted you in this way, "Hi! How <u>are</u> you?" And a true **Social** MEANS IT in asking. In fact, if you were to give a trivial response such as, "Oh, I'm fine. The reason that I have come to see you is…" Oh, no! We **Socials** would just not let you get away with that response. No. A true **Social** would not be able to do business with you until they have extracted an answer, thereby establishing a personal level exchange from which we would be comfortable to address the business reason for the visit.

Also, you have been able to spot a **Social** by watching them at a business meeting. We generally prefer to select a seat, let's say in a conference room, closest to the door. This is not in anticipation of being able to get out of the room first when the meeting is over. No, we just want to be seated conveniently to be able to greet everyone else who enters the room. This is our mission and we take it seriously, even if, mostly, unconsciously.

Now, we **Socials** do have a down-side, I'm afraid.

We have a VERY HIGH tolerance for ambiguity. Yes. We **Socials** have never been that concerned about completing things. For us, life has always been about the journey, not the arrival.

OPTIONS PEOPLE

Now these are very interesting folks. **OPTIONS** People are those who have ideas – all the time and about EVERYTHING. In fact, they tend to have one idea immediately after another. Often times the more recent ideas are contradictory to the previously stated ideas.

The interesting thing is that **OPTIONS** People see nothing wrong with expressing an idea on any topic, even though it may not be based in any set of facts whatsoever. Nope. They are just fine citing one idea and then another.

And here's where they add such significant value to any business thinking. **OPTIONS** People are the font of Creativity. They will think of new and unusual views of the same set of facts that you have already studied. And, **OPTIONS** People are fearless, unafraid of criticisms and very thick skinned.

In fact, at a problem-solving meeting, you could well turn to an **OPTIONS** Person after they have expressed an idea that is "way out there", and you could tell them, in front of everyone, that their last idea was the singularly least plausible solution that you have ever heard. And, here's how they will respond: "Oh, OK, how about if we were to try this other approach instead?"

You see, the time that you spent commenting on the **OPTIONS** Person's last idea, they were creatively formulating yet another way to approach the point. Oh, they are marvelous minds.

Next are **DETAILED** PEOPLE

DETAILED People are a set of folks living in their own world, usually. If you are reading this and you are a **DETAILED** Person, you know very well who you are.

And, I can tell everyone else who is reading that **DETAILED** People will "<u>Never Get Enough</u> – Detail, that is."

I used to call these folks, "The Drillers". That is because they will gladly drill down and drill down on any point or bit of minutia. And they will keep drilling down until someone stops them. As I said above, "They will never get <u>enough</u> detail."

These are very valuable folks to have on a work team, of course. These are the people who will question the "how" of every proposal for problem solutions. That is the way in which they are uniquely positioned to keep the problem-solving exercise in the realm of reality.

And, finally, there are the **CLOSURE** people.

I can best describe these folks as the people that you have certainly met who have a deep NEED for an ANSWER to EVERYTHING, and they need that answer NOW.

These **CLOSURE** folks have a very short fuse for conversation or discussion of a problem area. They want to get right to the solutions conversation – just as soon as possible and before most others have digested the breadth and their understanding of the problem itself.

And another thing, people of **CLOSURE** are the originators of the "Trial and Error" method of problem solving. Yes, they believe it is the best path to solutions by attempting one fix and seeing if it works. If it doesn't, they will come back, reconsider and try a different solution – and so forth until they have found the solution that solves the problem.

I should note that for **CLOSURE** folks, the **mortal sin** in life is **inaction**. And, they see <u>discussion</u>, for the most part, as <u>inaction</u> and therefor wasting valuable time. So, trying <u>any</u> way forward until the problem is solved is the most promising way to feel as though the problem is being addressed.

And these are <u>very valuable</u> folks to have on a work team. This is because these are the ones who have, for the most part, kept the rest of us behavioral style types <u>on task</u> throughout the years. I have come to appreciate them, and all the behavioral styles very much.

When I taught Team Building Skills to groups of young leaders over the past 20+ years, I pointed out that when forming the highest functioning, most successful team, it is best to be sure that each problem-solving team has at least one representative of each of the four Behavioral Styles. This will be, predictably, the most likely make up for success.

So, what does this have to do with Retirement?

Plenty, I think.

When we first Retire, many of us will have many choices for how to spend our time. Some will choose to work full time, some part time, and some will choose to volunteer their knowledge and skills to help others.

And here is the tie-in. In selecting things to do with our time, I recommend very strongly that we choose things that allow us to be OURSELVES. Find things that need us to operate in the way that is most natural for each of us. If we do this, we will be more comfortable and at ease (we're Retired – we <u>should</u> be "comfortable and at ease"!).

By way of example, I am a **Social** who has sought out and found outlets to <u>be with people</u> several times each month. I spend time at a local Veterans Center where I coach Vets in resume writing and preparation for interviews. Additionally, I deliver workshops and lectures, mostly at federal government agencies and a local university. I know that I <u>HAD</u> to do these things just to keep my sanity and joy. If I spent all my days in my little Retirement Cottage writing books and articles, I would just go nuts. I need people and I have searched them out. This is my nature, as a **Social**.

I know of a married couple who are clearly people of **OPTIONS** who retired at about the same time just a few years ago. They signed on with an organization called SCORE, a group, run by the Small Business Administration, whose purpose is the assist small businesses to start and prosper.

Once or twice a month, SCORE sponsors an open meeting for business owners to gather and share ideas in a non-competitive environment. SCORE has enlisted a panel of professionals who sit at the front of the meeting and who listen to the challenges of the attendees and offer ideas for ways forward.

The husband and wife are panelists at these meetings and their sole job is to listen to the business challenges being presented by the attendees and to offer ideas for solutions. Wow! Who better than an **OPTIONS** person?

These two folks are back in their element. And, they tell me, they will continue doing this for as long as SCORE will have them. They only do this once, maybe twice, a month. The rest of their time they are pursuing other activities that are on their "Bucket List". And, contrary to the idea that this activity is in any way a burden for them, they have told me that they look forward to the evenings when they will be on the panels and that they are thrilled to feel like their "old selves" again.

They tell me that they will continue this activity for as long as the organization will have them. This really rounds out their Retirement Activity Plan (more about this later).

Next example is a woman who retired after 32 years as a Financial Analyst for the civilian Department of the Navy. She was very clear that she fits the description of a **DETAILED** style.

After her Retirement on a Friday, she was coming out of her church the following Sunday when she met and shook hands with the Pastor. During this encounter, she whispered to the Pastor that she had just Retired and would have time, if the parish needed any help during the weeks to come.

The Pastor phoned her at home later to ask what kind of work she would most like to contribute. Remembering our discussion of this point in a workshop with me, she pointed out that she was a very **DETAILED** person and any needs for that kind of specialty would be of most interest.

The Pastor told her that he had been having a challenging time with the accounting for the parish and would love some help in that area. She pointed out that she was not a bookkeeper, but being **DETAILED,** she was sure that she could learn and contribute whatever was needed.

The following week she went to the Parish House Office, went over the accounts with the Pastor, and immediately saw where she could improve the process. Also, she signed up for a basic accounting course at her local community college to understand the nuances of the work.

Well, she told me that since then the Pastor no longer handles any of the financial matters. She comes to the Parish Office one afternoon per week (that's all!) and prepares the weekly deposit, and pays and posts the necessary bills. The outside auditor for the parish has reviewed all that she does and has been deeply complimentary.

Again, this fine lady told me that she loves doing this work because it allows her to be herself (**DETAILED**) and to be contributing to an organization that she loves. Her words to me, the last time that we communicated, were, "I'll do this for my parish for as long as they will have me".

And, finally, a woman who Retired for a federal agency came to see me. She was both a Lawyer and a CPA. But, she did not wish to do either of these jobs in her Retirement. We talked for a while about the parts of her jobs that she had most (and least) enjoyed and it was clear that she was a **CLOSURE** style person.

I recommended to her, and she followed through, to attend a local university for just a couple of courses and qualify for a Professional Certification as an Executive Coach.

She now has begun consulting to the senior executives of two non-profit organizations where she is teaching and coaching them in how to make good decisions during their work.

Well, who better that a **CLOSURE** person? And, again, this is something that she spends, at most, two days out of every month of Retirement pursuing. The rest of the time, she pursues her relaxing dream life.

This is the way it seems to work best. I recommend consideration of this point and adding it to the Retirement planning.

So, again, in selecting things to do with our time, I recommend very strongly that we choose things that allow us to be OURSELVES. Find things that need us to operate in the way that is most natural for each of us. If we do this, we will be more comfortable and at ease (we're Retired – we should be "comfortable and at ease"!).

Second: **Social Needs Traits**

You have probably noticed that there are some real differences in the needs of people for the company of others, or not.

Some folks have a strong need to be surrounded by others with constant interaction, or at least that interactions are available, whether accessed or not.

Then again there are those who will get along just fine if left to themselves. In many cases, these people <u>prefer</u> solitary daily life.

I do not believe that there is a "right" or "wrong" way to be. These are just plain differences in people and can be observed and acknowledged, requiring no judgements.

In fact, I have observed that there seems to be a continuum of preference in this matter where only a few people are to the extreme in either social need. At one end of the continuum, a person who has no need to be surrounded by others and in fact prefers to be alone, might be found. I would call this person a "Hermit".

At the opposite end of the spectrum we will find folks who are in deep need of company always and at all hours. They are disturbed by the prospect of being left alone and are just not sure how to operate when left to their own devices. I would refer to this person as a "Primary Social".

Here's how this Social Spectrum lays out:

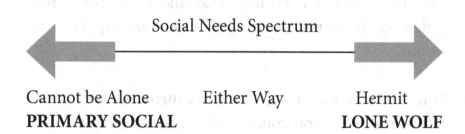

Social Needs Spectrum

Cannot be Alone   Either Way   Hermit
PRIMARY SOCIAL   **LONE WOLF**

Now, my assumption is that most of us are somewhere in between each extreme. The challenge is to pinpoint where we are on this spectrum.

How can we know where we are? This is usually best approximated by others who know us well and can draw on their experience, observing us over several years, to advise where they see us on this line.

To allow for biases, I would check with at least five or more folks and average where their observations place us.

Having done so, what does this have to do with Retirement?

I would use this as a guide to select where I will live, with whom I will live, and the locality of activities to the place where I will live most enjoyably.

Please remember, there is no judgement here. Neither end, nor anywhere in the middle of this spectrum, is any better or worse than the other. It just seems to me that making this personal preference reality a part of the equation about our Retirement plan will add to our enjoyment of the experience.

An example of this is myself. My Social Preference is somewhere to the left of the middle of the spectrum, but not very far left. My friends and family tell me that I am certainly not a "Hermit" but that I have proven myself quite adaptable to living by myself, primarily. So, I spend my days writing (as right now), reading, and practicing my Buddhist rituals and study. But, I very much enjoy visitors and the time that I can spend with them.

So, this recognition is a strong part of my Retirement life and I am delighted that I could carry out this part of my plan.

CHAPTER 14

When Should I Retire?

WHEN IS "ENOUGH" ACTUALLY "ENOUGH"?

THIS IS ONE of the thorniest decisions that we will have to make in the planning for our Retirement. These are the decisions about, "When <u>CAN</u> I Retire?" and "When <u>SHOULD</u> I Retire?". And, although these two questions are related, they have very different calculations and implications for the balance of our lives.

"When <u>CAN</u> I Retire?"

Wrestling with the most common question about Retirement planning, "When <u>CAN</u> I Retire?", is a straight forward, data driven consideration. It involves such things as knowing when our Retirement Program from our employer, our 401k's, our IRA's, Social Security, and assorted other financial plans will allow us to begin our Retirement based on their rules (chronological age vs. years of employment, for one), the amounts accumulated leading to the monthly incomes from each, the coverage under organizational health care or the coverage of Medicare. These are very measurable and assessing these (often with the assistance of a Financial Advisor) will allow us to pinpoint a date when we will be "able" to Retire in the future.

But, even with the seeming simplicity of these calculations, I would recommend the following self-exploration to gain a level of comfort about this matter. Please consider the **Concept of Enough.**

Here is what I mean. I will explain this concept using my own experience as an example.

When I realized that my health would not permit for me to return to work, post open heart surgery, I wrestled mightily with whether I would be able to Retire, at least financially.

Over the years, I had done the right things. I had maximized my contributions to all 401k's that were offered by all employers. Also, I had saved money to the federal limits in IRA's and other savings vehicles.

Once trying to assess where I might stand in the conundrum of Retirement "affordability", I went to visit with my Financial Advisor, as soon as my health would allow. I explained to him that I wanted to Retire immediately and that there would be no further contributions to any of the savings accounts or investments.

I asked him what to do with the amounts in each of my Retirement accounts and, with his advice and assistance, we liquidated them and purchased a Life Time Annuity.

Now, I should caution that many Financial professionals advise against Annuities. The reasons to avoid these are many, I'm told. But, in my situation, this was the most attractive to me for my primary concern: I wanted to be Retired for as many years as remain, and I want to feel that I will receive enough income over those years to support a reasonably comfortable life.

The Life Time Annuity that I purchased guaranteed a specific monthly payment for the rest of my life. That was what I wanted.

I was told that I had a choice between two monthly amounts. The higher amount was a plan that would run out once my principal investment was used up (approximately age 92, if I remember correctly). My thinking was, though, suppose I live beyond 92? In my family that is very possible. What would I do then?

So, the lesser monthly payment that I agreed to was guaranteed by a company of long standing and with very deep pockets – to last past age 92 and continue for as long as I live. Now that is what I felt comforted by, all arguments to the contrary notwithstanding.

Additionally, I will tell you that on that very afternoon after meeting with my Financial Advisor and signing up for the annuity to begin immediately, I was driven to my local Social Security Administration office.

There, I went up to the counter and asked for my federal annuity (Social Security) to begin as soon as possible.

The very professional person who met with me there explained that at my then current age (62) I was certainly qualified for the beginning of payments. However, she explained, if I would choose to wait until age 66 (funny, I had thought for years that the magic age was 65, but that had changed for my "vintage", the payment that I would receive would be nearly 30% higher an amount, a significant difference. She also explained that if I would wait until age 70, the amount would be even higher.

I thanked her for this advice. I knew that she was certainly correct.

But, remember, I had just gone through Open Heart surgery and thus knew that my health is more fragile than I had previously realized. I could not afford to assume that I would live to be 66, let alone 70.

You know how much you get if you die prior to taking any payment from the Social Security Trust Fund? NOTHING! That's how much. Yes, after all my years of working and having FICA deductions removed from my pay, I would get not a dime of it back. Too bad for me!

So, I considered these facts, and said to the nice person at Social Security that I would take it now and feel very good about it.

In fact, I said to her that, using the phrase that she had just used to explain the larger amounts by waiting, "Well, it seems to me that the amount that Social Security pays me each month, starting immediately, is, in fact, 100% more than it is paying to me now."

And, with that, I thanked her for her professionalism and filled out the rest of the paperwork.

Now, let me ask you this: do you suppose that the combined amount of monthly payment from the both annuities equated to the net of my paycheck from my job as an executive at a Fortune 100? You are correct, not even close to the net.

And here is a major point that I would like to give you:

Although I would be living on a lesser amount of income each month, I believed then and now that the amount that I would be, and am receiving was and is **ENOUGH**.

This is a concept, **ENOUGH**, that is certainly necessary for any of us to come to grips with, if we are to choose to Retire, well, ever.

I know that we have grown up and attached ourselves, for the most part, to a contrary concept which has probably been helpful to us over the years. That concept has been the concept of **MORE**.

Sure, we were weaned on the concept of **MORE**. All through our lives, we came to equate "success" with this concept. Once we achieved any level for which we strove, a higher salary, a promotion, a bonus, or any additional recognition at work, we already knew that we desired yet another achievement - **MORE**.

This was a cycle and reality that, perhaps, served us well to motivate harder work, and attention to matters that would serve the outcome of **MORE**.

But to be able to squarely look at the prospect of a life without and substantial six-figure income, I was challenged to find out what was my "livable" financing monthly.

To arrive at this, I looked closely at several months of expenditures in my budget. I separated each line item into one of two columns. I titled one column, "Need" and the other one "Want". When I was done, I tabulated the "Need" column, added a few dollars for unanticipated financial needs, and I could identify the precise number that would be **ENOUGH**.

I felt very confident of this number and compared it to the total of my expected annuities, when combined. I was delighted to find that the income that I would enjoy exceeded the amount that I now knew would be **ENOUGH**.

I hope that you can see that this exercise was critical to be confident of my decision to Retire and be able to pay my way into the future. I highly recommend this process to all who consider whether they will be able to Retire. Without this calculation (and remember to add a bit for the unknowns), it is unlikely that we can be sure that we "can" retire.

And, as a note, I have held my spending to the level that I calculated. I have been quite conscious about this. There have been several challenges to my spending plan such as relatives needing financial help (mostly my kids) and the temptation to take an unnecessary trip or two.

Now, this is not to say that I haven't loaned (given) money to my son or taken a trip from time to time for fun and adventure. But I paid for these out of incidental income that has come from my writing and honorariums for my speaking engagements.

What I have been sure to do, though, is to not include the incidental income amounts into my budget equations, and for a very sound reason. I cannot predict the life of those sources of extra income. I cannot count on those and perceive my spending ability to be greater and, easily, do something foolish – like take on a larger home with costs above my currently budgeted amount.

There was one other change that I made in this financial area. I sold my home shortly after Retirement.

I had lived for years in a large home in a wealthy suburb of Washington, DC. I used to call it, "The Mansionette". It was very nice, to be sure. It sat on a very large lot with a large front lawn, a circular driveway, and a swimming pool in the back, of course. It has 5 bedrooms and 4 bathrooms. But I was, by then, living there alone. It was just too much house for one person and I recognized that the expenses associated with upkeep and taxes were unsustainable without a big executive salary.

So, I made the decision to sell the house and downsize into a more modest home – one more appropriate for a single person of more modest means. And here's how I made peace with this decision.

I realized that my goal to live my dream of Retirement – living modestly, writing books (like this one), and speaking before audiences from time to time – was a treasured way of living that I would have to sacrifice some things to accomplish. So, deciding to sell the house was just a step along the way and I decided to just sell it and not look back.

Well, I put the house on the market at the bottom of the market in late 2008. Yes, the very worst time to have sold real estate.

But, it sold quickly at the only Open House that the realtor held – to the second couple who walked through that day. And do you suppose that the amount that the folks offered was what I had asked? In 2008's market, not a chance.

But, do you know what the offer, which I accepted, was? It was **ENOUGH**! Yes, it was **ENOUGH** so that I was able, at the closing table, to pay what needed to be paid. And there was **ENOUGH** left over after that to be able to go to a local Retirement Village and purchase a condominium with two bedrooms, two bathrooms, a living room, separate dining room, kitchen, laundry room, and a glass enclosed balcony that was an additional room. And all of this, I was happy with because it was **ENOUGH**.

This was another application of the concept of **ENOUGH** and I am quite delighted to have been able to consciously choose the conditions that have allowed me to Retire and live my dream life.

"When SHOULD I Retire?"

This is the trickiest question of all.

It involves a lot of moving parts and is extremely personal, a unique answer for each person that asks the question. And we all, eventually, answer this question for ourselves based on the criteria that feels right for us.

The included questions, necessary to be confident of our eventual answer are many, but at least these:

1. What role does my family's desires and needs play in deciding this?
2. What options should I consider with my supervisor in selecting the best time to go?
3. Similarly, what about colleagues? What considerations should I give to their projects and needs?
4. And, in the end, how will I feel right about selecting a time to go?

Here are my thoughts about how to consider these matters.

1. What role does my family's desires and needs play in deciding this?

Of course, family dynamics and relationships vary greatly, so I can only suggest a thought here that applies where appropriate.

It is rare that any profound change in one's life affects only the individual experiencing the change. For most, our family is an extension of our own life and our good and bad fortunes will affect each of the members of our family to differing degrees and, perhaps, in diverse ways.

This is because our family is a social organization and we are interconnected regardless of our intentions. What affects one, affects all.

Let me give an example. When we announce to our adult children that we (our self and our partner) have decided to Retire, what they HEAR is, quite often, "Oh, Boy! Babysitters are becoming available – free babysitters, at that! Now we can take week long vacations, just my partner and me, and leave the kids in safe hands with Gramps! Hooray!"

I'll suggest some cautions for this example a little later, but the point here is that everyone in our family that we tell of our decision to Retire will assess the announcement in relation to its meaning in their own lives. This is usually a good thing, but my point remains that being clear with our family about our plans and timing for Retirement will impact the family in some way.

Having written that, it seems clear that our ability to enjoy our years of Retirement are directly connected to the amount of cooperation, interplay, and support that members of our family will provide.

Particularly, as we age, we will need more and more help just with the simplest tasks of daily living. And, although resources are available in most communities for these supportive assistances, for many of us the family will want to chip in their help in varying degrees. I would go beyond saying that this is a good thing. The family support for our later years is a part of any family's journey and the degree of active participation continues (and grows) generation over generation.

2. What options should I consider with my supervisor in selecting the best time to go?

This suggestion is more than a matter of common courtesy.

Perhaps it's because I spent much of my career in the Human Resources activities of organizations that I feel strongly about this matter. This is because I have seen the coordination done well (by both the boss and the soon-to-be Retiree) and not-so-well and I have observed the consequences of each.

Our supervisors are responsible for the smooth operation of our group to include task assignments and the prudent use of resources. They rely on assumptions about their work force to make the smartest decisions. One of the most common assumptions is the size and availability of all members of their team.

Now, I have heard from some folks, when I shared my thinking above, that they don't understand why the boss' problems should be theirs. I don't think that all people would react this way, but some do. So, here's my encouragement about this.

Please remember that while in a job we have been contributing, to the best of our ability, towards the meeting and exceeding of both personal and group goals. The accomplishment of the group's goals has provided us with both an income as well as a pride of participation and accomplishment that has meant something to us for many years of our work life.

At the end of our job these feelings of accomplishment and pride have formed a legacy that will be memorable for those left at the job site and for our own sense of contribution.

And, of course, the notion of "Knowledge Transfer" is of concern to so many that I have coached through the Retirement experience – the person Retiring, their leaders, their peers, and subordinates.

Here the key question revolves around the passing of institutional knowledge, project knowledge, and insights gained over the years of team work. These will function as the "oil" to allow successors to optimize their own efforts, confident with the insights of those who came before, not simply replicating errors to learn ways forward, but applying the historical learning from those who proceeded.

This is a responsibility that not all have recognized intuitively. But, upon discussion and reflection, so many have thanked me for guiding them in this level of human camaraderie and responsibility to the tasks and accomplishments of those who others will follow.

This flow of knowledge connects generations of professionals with similar goals and dreams. The past influences the present and assures a better future result for the organization's goals.

Personally, I believe that this is worth consideration. It may be true that once "out the door", the success or failure of the group is on them, not us. But, I know folks who have had regrets when looking back on their last months and, even, days on the job.

I know that it has been a source of pride for me to look back and rest well knowing that I gave it my all until the very last moment and that no one should have felt that I let them down in any way. This cannot always be accomplished, but working on a "game plan" with our supervisor (some call this their "exit strategy") that encompasses both a timing and a to-do list that we can check off to be confident of a smooth transition of all work to those who succeed us.

3. Similarly, what about colleagues? What considerations should I give to their projects and needs?

Please see my answer to number two, above.

I would add here that my colleagues, my fellow workers over the years have formed a team environment that I operated as a part to accomplish goals and meet organizational expectations. I sincerely have wanted these folks to feel that I gave a 100% effort until the very end. I wanted them to remember me fondly after my departure, not begrudging things and responsibilities that I added to their existing workloads.

When my name is mentioned at each organization, I have done all that I can to ensure that they will remember that I was a team player until the very last day and hour. This is a legacy. Legacies can be either positive or negative in quality. It has been my preference that these legacies be the very best when referring to me. I rest just a little bit more comfortably in my rocker, looking out the back of my Retirement home at the slowly meandering river, as I think of my colleagues and my contributions to our common cause.

4. And, in the end, how will I feel right about selecting a time to go?

And now we get to the most important manner of thinking about the right time in my life for me to invoke my Retirement.

I believe two things that seem to be crucial.

First, I have never been an advocate of "Running Away" from anything or situation. This just doesn't seem to ever be successful. In fact, what usually seems to happen is that whatever negativity caused us to want to run in the first place, will reappear in the place to which we run.

I am quite sure that this is because the Universe operates systematically by the Law of Cause and Effect. What I mean is that most any situation in which I have found myself during my 70 years of life was invariably caused to happen by me – somewhere along the line. That does not ring true for many, but it's my truth.

On a profound level, all my life situations – "good" and "bad" – have been either caused by my actions or they have been <u>allowed</u> to happen by me, in some way. This is part of my view of all of life as a 100% Responsibility sum game. I have developed a belief that I am the author of my life and my destiny. I create all the variables, even those that seem to be random.

There are no "co-incidences". There you have it. And, I realize that many will part company with me here holding on to a world view of determinism and vulnerability where each of us is at the mercy of forces outside of ourselves and/or seemingly randomness.

Well, you are, of course, welcome to your view of the world. Now you know a slice of mine.

Secondly, I am not an advocate of making a change for the sake of change.

In other words, if things in our job are going well and we are pleased with our work life as it is; and, if there are no other causes, such as failing health of our self or loved ones who need care, then I see no need to rush head long into Retirement for the sake of an arbitrary date.

And there are other considerations.

Let's assume that we are financially prepared to Retire.

And let's assume that our family (spouse/partner) is on the same page and is ready to enjoy Retirement.

There is a way to look at some tangible interpersonal assessments that can help us to be clear about the timing of our Retirement.

In sum, a trusted friend and colleague advised me, as I pondered my final decision to Retire. She said, simply, **PAY ATTENTION**. But, **PAY ATTENTION** to what?

Here are the three areas for consideration and the questions to ask about each. The answers, very personal indeed, will certainly inform our thinking about the timing of our entry into our Retirement journey.

In each of these three areas, ask ourselves these two questions: "What do I see changing?" "How does that make me feel?"

Here's the first:

Of course, all organizations change over time. Some get larger or smaller. Operations become more and differently technical utilizing often recent technologies and other Systems. The leadership changes both immediately and at the top levels. And, yes, often the Mission of the organization changes. It has different goals and measures of success than what existed when we joined the organization.

These have impacts on us that will be measured from small to large. I'm suggesting that we take the time to tease out the nuances of what is changing in our organization and reflect on how what we observe makes us feel.

Here is my example.

My last job before Retirement was as a Vice President of Human Resources with a Fortune 100 company. My specialty was the communication and retention of employees during mergers and acquisitions.

In fact, I was specifically hired by that company because they had recently acquired several small companies and they were in the process of assimilating the employees of those acquired firms into the larger company. However, and it is not unusual at all, the acquiring company was witnessing a significant exodus of the most talented employees. Interestingly, the talents that the departing employees possessed were among the most attractive aspects of purchasing those businesses.

I had a great deal of experience in identifying the reasons that employees "jump ship" when new ownership arrives. And, my track record was one of the best for being able to assess and remedy the percentage of employees who would leave, thus restricting what was dubbed, "the talent drain".

Well, as I have described in an earlier chapter, after just a couple of years of my employment there, my boss took me aside and shared that the company had made a strategic decision to hold off on acquisitions or mergers for the foreseeable future. This was based on business strategies that I fully understood.

This turn of events, however, would leave me with only a limited number of options for internal transfer to maintain my vice president's level and pay. Also, the only upcoming appropriate openings were what is known as "line" Human Resources jobs, not utilizing my expertise. And, none of the target jobs was located near my home town, but on the other side of the U. S.

So, the above couple of paragraphs describes the "what" that was going on in my organization.

How that made me feel was: great anxiety. I would need to move away from my comfort zones of expertise and physical location. I did not wish to do either of these things. And, I should mention, the market need for my expertise was very limited and I did not think that I would find another job readily in my field.

So, that's just one example. What are your responses?

The next area of consideration is:

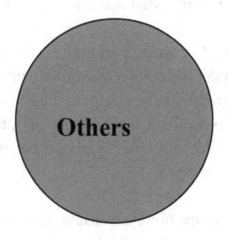

This is an area to consider that will have varying differences in importance to each of us. Here is the thing to notice.

Of course, over the years, the people who work with us, and for us, and for whom we work, have changed. The individuals with whom we have worked have changed (everyone does, even in the smallest of ways) and a newer/younger generation or two of workers have joined the ranks of our workplace along the way.

The key observation is to notice the ways in which people's habits, work processes, abilities, knowledge, and so forth may differ from what we have become accustomed. Note those things that strike us as different, perhaps a new "normal". And then, for each observation, let's ask ourselves: "How does that make me feel?"

The way that changes in the people around us at work impact us will range from enthusiastic approval, even "refreshing", to annoying and all gradations in between.

This is just the normal way of things. Changes happen and we have a reaction to those changes. But, it has never been more helpful to focus on the reality of our work life and make honest assessments about how we are responding to those new realities.

For some of us, perhaps, we will total up the "score" of our reactions to the changes around us and we will be delighted and encouraged to stay at what we are doing for a while longer. Others of us may not be so willing to stay if there is a sense that so much is different in the way that people around us at work are acting and interacting with us and it is causing us stress on a constant basis.

My assessment was the later.

For the last several years of my career, I was noticing behaviors and styles of communicating by fellow workers that became progressively more distracting and I felt increasingly like an "old fogy".

I noticed, for example, the ways in which younger male team members seemed to put less and less care into choosing what to wear to work, personal grooming (such as shaving – always a "five O'clock Shadow"? Even at 8 AM at the office? How is that even possible? Well, now I began to see myself as "old school" and I wasn't happy with that label.

And then there was the change in style of working that puzzled me increasingly. By this I mean the change in communication mediums. For example, everyone in the younger set seemed to only desire to communicate by way of emails and texts. And, the abilities of younger employees to communicate either in person or by composing a coherent written statement was far from snuff. Oh, this last one shocked me to observe even from new hires that we recruited from graduate schools. Well, my feelings about this will be the subject, perhaps, of later books.

But, most pertinent to this point is that I assessed the impact of these kinds of observations on me. And, I did not like the perceived level of stress that all of this added up to for me. The observations of changed behavior were so pervasive and I did not see a "fix". This caused stress, though I was not so sure that these changes were necessarily "bad", but boy were they different.

I know, of course, that this phenomenon of human change has always been afoot. It was true when my generation (combination of "love children" and Viet Nam Veterans) came into the work force. And we caused change to happen in time, much of which turned out to render improvements on the organizations that we served.

So, I'm not wishing to pass judgement on the kinds of changes in the work force that surrounds us, but to recommend that seeing the differences and, more importantly, **paying attention** to how these changes make each of us feel, informs an assessment of whether this aspect suggests that it is time to Retire or, perhaps, wait just a bit longer if we are enjoying the changes that we see.

Which brings us to the last and most thorny area for consideration: Our Selves.

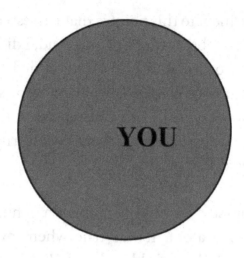

For me, this was the most difficult area to look at and assess honestly – even to myself.

But, in fact, I had been noticing things about my abilities changing, even ever so gradually over time. I started noticing changes in my late 50's and I wrote off most of what I saw as just quirks and unimportant to who I was. But, by the time I was in my early 60's, I found myself constantly frustrated, particularly by my cognitive ability.

I had enjoyed a lifetime of unusually clear memory and it had served me well. Particularly in High School, in undergraduate school, and in graduate school.

I had an "autogenic" memory. That is, if I heard something I would remember it for at least the next six months. I mean, I would remember a statement exactly as it was said with the words used and the inflections of the speaker.

You can imagine. Everyone in school wanted to study with me when preparing for an exam. If the instructor had said something during the semester, I was the one who would always remember the instructor's precise wording. Getting top grades was, of course, a snap for me.

Yes, I rose quickly in business and was known as the one executive who could attend a meeting and not need to take notes. If it was said, I got it and kept it in my treasured mind.

And, then, when I turned from my 50's into my 60's, it was gone. I could no longer remember even the simplest of things, never mind details.

To say the least, this was frustrating to me and difficult to accept.

I suspected that I might have "early on set" Alzheimer's disease. I went through rigorous testing at Johns Hopkins University Hospital. The initial testing was inconclusive and they prescribed a course of Aricept which at that time was the Gold Standard for memory drugs.

A few months later, I was tested again and this time the doctors concluded that my experience was most likely not a product of a disease state but a natural devolution of my memory ability. It would not improve, but would likely get more problematic over the years.

This was a hard pill to swallow for me, as you can imagine.

But, here's the bottom line about this for me.

At the point that all of this sunk in for me, I realized that here I was holding down (as best I could) a very senior position in a huge company where my bosses, my staff, and all the employees counted on me to provide the very best advice and counsel in matters of Human Resources management. But I was less and less able, over a short amount of time, to provide more than the minimum of responses. I was spending long amounts of time in my office and worrying about the next knock on my door and whether I would be able to rise to whatever occasioned the knock.

In sum, I felt that I was no longer earning the very hefty salary that I was receiving. The company was simply not getting its money's worth and this was an awesome burden on my conscience.

As I considered my options, securing another job at a rival company was an option, perhaps. But, then I would still be in the same spot once the "honeymoon effect" of new employment wore off.

So, how did this make me feel? Lousy, for sure.

The amount of stress that this was causing me daily was enormous, as you can imagine.

For me, this was the deciding factor to initiate my Retirement journey.

Finally, I would add that when reviewing all three of the areas of consideration, Organization, Others, and Self, my decision for the timing of my Retirement was one that I made with confidence – even relief.

I hope that this is helpful for you to add to the calculus for selecting the best timing for you journey.

CHAPTER 15

Retirement Planning

PLANNING

Welcome to your planning for your career retirement. There's no question that this is a move into uncharted waters with the feeling that once begun, there's no turning back. While it is easy to forget, you *have* been in this change predicament before, and you have survived all that has come along!

Don't just SURVIVE – THRIVE

CARPE DIEM – Seize The Day – Live today like there's no tomorrow! Let yourself appreciate *every* moment of this day – this one, right now. No looking back and no pining for some future day to come. Learn this ability – you'll be the happiest person in the world – every day of your life.

And, remember: We retire from our careers, but there's **NO** "retirement" from life. Live **EVERY** DAY and enjoy what there is to enjoy. We have so much to be grateful for with every breath we take. This is our next goal: Joie de vie! Let's acquire it and hold fast to it for the balance of our days.

I SUSPECT THE reason you are reading this book today is that you find yourself thinking about your future – beyond work. You will find that most of the published materials about "Retirement" that are found in research and on search engines, are solely about the financial side of retirement. This presupposes that the only thing that counts is the ability to pay your bills and financially survive after you stop working.

I value these monetary guidelines; but they only address the question: "When **CAN** I retire?" (Please see pages 242 and 243 for some thoughts on this.)

I am more concerned with the question: "When **SHOULD** I retire?" I consider this to be a much more subjective question since it requires us to think about and plan so many factors that will affect the day-to-day enjoyment of our time and life, once we take the retirement plunge. Personally, I found this to be the thornier question since answering it required me to think through my life plan and to adopt goals and, in my case, a persona that was new for me, and quite pleasurable. Please see pages 242 through 266 for an in-depth set of ideas about the "Should" of Retirement Planning. Let's focus on **Re-Invention**.

This is a good point at which to restate my story. This is important because my experience certainly informs my views of the preparation for retirement far more than the considerable research that I have done. Throughout this book, I have referred to my own retirement experience – getting it started, deciding how to proceed, and now enjoying every single day.

Yes, I AM retired. Oh, I am involved in so many things day-to-day that you'd think that I must be employed. But, I am spending my time now <u>the way I **want** to spend it</u> and the way that I **planned** it.

Let me take you through my Retirement experience, step by step.

I spent most of my career in both public and private organizations working in the field of Human Development (Leadership, Talent Management, Change Management (transitions), Performance Enhancement, Quality of Life, and Mediation). Essentially, I was always involved in the endeavor to assist all levels of an organizational community to learn how to talk to each other – in respectful, effective, and meaningful ways.

In early 2008, I was a Vice President with a Fortune 100 corporation, overseeing Human Resources for several hundred new employees who were assimilating into the larger organization from several smaller companies that had been recently acquired. This project, however, was coming to an end and I was summoned to the corporate headquarters to meet with the Senior Vice Presidents to explore options for my next assignment.

You probably know from your own experience that the higher up in an organization that you get, the fewer the options – because there are only so many vice presidents, even in a mega-organization. So, I was not surprised to learn that there would only be two openings that rated a vice president over the following eighteen months.

Both jobs were "plant-level" (meaning management of an HR team supporting several thousand employees at a single plant site) and both were in very rural areas in the South Western United States. I didn't really have to give too much thought to these options since Plant-Level HR was not a logical next step for my communications expertise, and, well, I am from the East Coast of the U. S. I cannot even imagine myself living in a rural area, much less in a desert-like environment. No Thanks.

So, naturally, I asked the question: "What's behind Door #3"?

After some heavy silence, the boss said, "Well, you could always leave…"

This option had already occurred to me, of course. I knew several things:

Although the senior executive employment market was slowing considerably, I had great credentials and wonderful references. I was confident that a major corporation would hire me within a few months.

1. I had only just turned age 62. Now, I was no spring chicken, but I was well within the normal age group for vice presidents, certainly within major organizations.
2. I sure did have a retirement plan, but I had figured to jump into that life stage once I was at least 65 to 67 (my Financial Advisor used to regularly emphasize

age 70 to maximize retirement income, overcoming some failed investments from earlier in life – but what did he know?).

3. Also, before retiring, my plan included finishing my PhD, at long last, and teaching some courses in the day school of the university where I had been an adjunct for a few years, teaching as a substitute and in the weekend and evening schools. Hence, a huge part of my plan was to find a professorship somewhere, get tenure, and live out my days in the Halls of Ivy, waxing philosophically. Oh, this was a great part of my dream!

4. I should add that my plan included the vision of me living the quiet life of a scholar, in a small English-village style home, with roaring fireplaces. There I would write books (a lifelong hobby has been writing, but never a book, just short stories and professional articles for journals), and prepare my lectures.

So, I skewed up my courage and said that I would leave.

This was, of course, after all the assessing of my life and realities that I discussed in the previous chapter.

My boss and I agreed to a severance plan giving me several months to land elsewhere and I would leave graciously. I returned home that evening feeling very satisfied with the outcome.

And, then, as is so often the case, life happened.

The very day after my return from the meeting at Corporate Headquarters, I was sitting in my office planning how to best wrap up the project and effect an orderly turnover of various matters.

At about mid-day, I began to feel sick in a way that I had never felt before. Now, this was unusual for me because I happen to be one of those people in this world who, until then, had bragging rights that I had not been sick a day in my life (a little head cold here and there, but that's all), no broken bones, no close calls, just as healthy as a horse. At 300+ pounds, this would be a Clydesdale horse, of course, but a horse none-the-less.

But, on this afternoon, I was experiencing pains in the front of my chest and more sharply on my upper left side and it extended down my left shoulder and the top of the arm.

This was so strange for the ever healthy me that I decided to just ignore it, try to concentrate on my work and wait for it to pass. But it didn't.

After some time, one of the members of my staff came into my office to talk to me about something. She took one look at me and picked up the phone and dialed 9-1-1.

The emergency folks got their rapidly and whisked me onto a rolling stretcher (no small task at my size – I felt sorry for them) and rolled me to the elevator and to the waiting ambulance.

One thing that I can share with you about this part of the experience is that leaving work in this fashion is extremely ungracious – no clever remarks to the on-lookers came to mind so I just smiled at everyone and waved.

Later that night, still in the Emergency Room at the hospital, a cardiology physician came in to see me and told me what their many tests had discovered.

He said that there was a mixture of good news and not so good news. It seemed that I was having a "heart event", and that it was not over yet. On the one hand, they had determined that I had experienced a very mild stroke, but that its effects seemed minimal with no evidence of paralysis or slurring, and if there would be any, it would have started by then.

He went on to say that there was more.

He reminded me (as though I could EVER forget) that earlier in the afternoon a group of doctors had run a tiny camera through an artery at the top of my leg and threaded it to my heart to look around. Here, again, they found both good and not so good news. What they found was a deterioration of my aortic heart valve. With a little more time of non-detection, that would have burst and ended my life.

The good news, he said, was that because of the stroke, they had cause to investigate and catch this "silent killer" in time to act. He explained that this problem was quite common and could be fixed with a fairly routine procedure. They would need to replace my valve and clean things up, but I would be able to live a normal life span, with any luck at all.

Of course, I agreed to the procedure and they scheduled the surgery for a couple of days later (must have been a big month for aortic valves in that heart unit). Then, to my surprise the doctor offered to discharge me with my promise to return in the wee hours of the day of the surgery for preparation.

I asked how this was possible and he explained that there was no advantage to me to stay at the hospital for the next couple of days. It seems that if a valve is going to cease to function, the patient being at home or in a hospital makes no difference, and there was no reason to believe that my condition would deteriorate for at least another month or more. I accepted the "hall pass" and went home.

Now, here's where you come in. You see, while I was riding home in a taxi that night (wee early hours), I was deep in thought. I wondered to myself, "How could this have happened?" Oh, I don't mean about the stroke or even the bad valve, which could happen to anyone. I asked myself how it was possible that I could have lived for 62 years and NOT have prepared one bit for my death.

As incredible as it seemed to me at the time, I realized that I had not prepared in any way to die. My "affairs" were in complete disarray.

I did not have a valid Will. Without that, in my state (Maryland), the probate courts apply "in testate" laws and divide the dead person's assets in keeping with the State's formulae. This is not OK with me, but my inaction had put my estate in a passive state where my wishes would not be followed.

Also, I had never created a Living Will, which would tell my health care providers about my wishes if my health were deteriorating, and I was unable to communicate. It would specify the levels of care and extraordinary measures that I would want as my health condition changed. This would leave the matter up to my "next of kin" and the doctors. But, these would not be considering <u>my</u> wishes, so my silence condemned me to their best "guess".

And, as well, I realized that my finances were in virtual disarray. Oh, I knew where everything was located, but I have no idea how anyone else would find the resources and assets to supply for an accounting of my estate, or, for that matter, to assist me financially should I be alive but non-communicative. I had lived alone for over 20 years and no one was versed in the whereabouts of my estate.

Does any of this sound familiar?

And, if you are asking yourself the question that I posed above (How did this happen?), I wonder how you would answer that question, if similarly posed?

For me, the answer was painful but obvious. I had assumed that I WAS IMMORTAL! Yes, of course I had. Oh, I had never said this out loud (they generally put you behind padded walls for those kinds of statements). But, as always, my behavior had betrayed my beliefs.

I had not done a thing because I was in denial that I would someday end up as ALL before me had – I will die. There. I've said it.

This was a bitter pill. You see, I've tried to spend my life with openness and candor. I've tried to face every situation head-on without looking away. And, most of all, I've spent a life trying, as best I could, to avoid the "drama" that seems to plague the lives of many others.

But here I was, realizing that by not being prepared for death, or debilitation that would leave me unable to communicate and care for myself, I was allowing a murky situation to unfold for those in my family who would want to help. This would lead to drama – it always does – perhaps infighting and disagreements about how to care for me or how to dispose of my belongings and, even, body.

One of my favorite professors, in graduate school at Johns Hopkins University, had a wonderful saying, "Where there is *trauma*, there will always be *drama*."

Wow, have I ever lived to see the truth in that quip. Haven't you? It does seem that when there's acute and traumatic events in a family, such as the illness or imminent death of a loved one, the surrounding family can slip into sharp disagreements based on "fuzzy memories". You have probably seen this too.

And, I don't want this to happen in my family, surrounding my health or looming death. I recognize that it is **my** responsibility to avoid, as much as possible, this kind of rancor when I'm sick and, eventually, dying.

This is the person that I want to be. So, I decided that the two-day reprieve before the operation would need to be spent taking care of my "affairs" – so I got busy.

During the next couple of days, I accomplished three major objectives:

1. I created a Last Will and Testament
2. I executed a Living Will
3. I incorporated my wishes for what I wanted at every stage of my remaining life into a contract – entered with my closest family members (brothers, sisters, and son) and I titled this my "Care Contract"

I'll go into some detail about each of these in the following pages. If you haven't done this preparation for yourself and you feel inspired to change that, I'll also tell you how to secure a copy of these documents (without my personal details, of course – a little too personal) very easily and these will give you a place to start.

A LAST WILL AND TESTAMENT

It is embarrassing for me, in retrospect, to admit that I had lived for over 60 years at that point without creating a Will (*Last Will and Testament*). Oh, I had written down basic wishes on a one-page document that was distributed while my Marine Unit was waiting to depart for the Far East in 1971. This was a Will, they told us, and it was required of all of us 20-somethings before we would be allowed to enter the tarmac and onto the jet to take us East, many for the very last time.

I still have a copy of that document (somewhere), but it contains the names and basic addresses for people who are, mostly, long since dead and many names that I don't even recognize – probably whoever I smoked the last bowl with. If you are near my age, you know what that means. If not, ignore, please.

In any event, we should all know by now that to die without having executed a legal Will (this is called, "*In Testate*") means that the disposition of our estate will be decided solely by a judge in our last state of residence. Our preferences and wishes do not count and that's just not a turn of events that I desired.

So, I contacted a lawyer and explained that I had just a little time to create this document before "going under the knife". Without time to set up an appointment in his office, the lawyer walked me through the wording and listing of my assets, over the phone. He asked his assistant to join the call and write up the document based on my wishes.

The document was completed and sent to my home the next day with a couple of my neighbors (witnesses) in tow. This made it legal and one thing that I could check from my list.

And, here I would recommend that a lawyer in your state will be the best resource for creating this necessary document. I know that there are web sites now that purport to legally create a document for you at very low cost. I cannot and I am not qualified to vouch for the certainty of this route. Many have said that this is a far less expensive way to have a Will created.

I leave this to your judgement. A simple Google© Search will provide ample alternatives and prices. In fact, as a test, I recently typed in, "Low Cost Last Will for Maryland (exchange for your State)" and I found a site that would produce a Will, guaranteed to pass muster in my State for just under $100.00.

A LIVING WILL

Now this document is one that, today, is required before we will be admitted to a hospital. It is a very important document, of course, for reasons that follow.

Let me repeat what I stated about this document just a few pages ago.

A Living Will, informs our health care providers about our wishes when health is deteriorating, and we are unable to communicate. It specifies the levels of care and extraordinary measures that we want as our health condition changes. This leaves the matter up to my "next of kin" (also known as our designated Health Care Power of Attorney (person that we designate to make decisions about our health when we are unable to communicate) and the doctors.

Even so, this document is about my wishes for medical care late in life. But, as for when the end is at hand, the stipulations in the standard Living Will document leaves all of the decision process about cessation of care and Do Not Resuscitate (DNR) instructions entirely on the conscience of my Power of Attorney designee without the benefit of <u>my own</u> wishes.

My silence condemns my designee and my family to their best "guess".

Note: I have known friends who have been the designee for older loved ones and, at some point, the medical team asked them for a decision to continue or to terminate "extraordinary measures" (keeping the loved one alive, no matter what). And here's the damnable thing, several of those friends have shared with me that even many years after the loved one's death, the designee questions their decision. They have said to me, "I just don't know. Did I decide too quickly and maybe she could have survived?" Or, "Did I wait too long and he suffered unnecessarily?"

Of course, these are unanswerable questions; yet, questions that will potentially stick with the designee and family for a lifetime.

Then, too this Living Will does not address my wishes for how to provide care for me as I age. Hopefully, long prior to my death. And I felt that this is an area of my preferences that would require decisions and actions on the part of my family. I owe them my guidance here, in advance of each step or stage.

Really, what I most want is to be sure that my family has a Road Map for how I would like my living arrangements and care to proceed as my life unfolds. Yes, I know who I am and what my values and wishes are.

Yet, I knew, as I reviewed my relationship and history with my family, that I had never really sat down with them to explain my aging and care plan.

Here's a resource for a place to start a Living Will: www. legalnature.com/**LivingWill**

Passive Aging

Have you noticed this in your community, too?

It seems that most of my contemporaries (folks in their 60's and beyond) seldom take the time to stipulate what they will want at each stage of their elderly years. Yes, they just seem to continue to live, age, and, of course, grow ill, feeble, and less able to care for themselves. And they let this occur and virtually wait to see what those around them are going to do to help them. As though life is to be lived passively.

Well, I decided that my life would not unfold this way (passively). I decided that it was critical to step up, on my own behalf. And, it seemed critical to do this within weeks of this realization. Why? Well, I figured then that I will never be as mentally agile again. Aging involves a dimming of cognition, under the best of circumstances.

So, I felt that it was best to write down my wishes while I was still young enough to think through what I wanted and valued. Then I would share this with my family – **in writing**, so that all knew what I desired.

Oh, "in writing" is very important in my view. Here's why.

Have you noticed that in times of crisis (*trauma* leading to *drama*), people's memories get very fuzzy? The arguments that ensue are predictable ("I know him very well and I know what he would have wanted at this point") and that statement flies in the face of everyone else's memories…

Well, that's why I opted to put my wishes into writing. This became a multi-page document that I titled, **"My Care Contract"**. See the next chapter for details about this document and its usefulness.

And now: **What about your Retirement Activity Planning?**

Long before I Retired, I had formulated a "dream" of who I would become once Retired.

I was inspired by the life of one of my literary heroes, Samuel Clemens (Mark Twain). Clemens spent the bulk of his adult life writing books and traveling the world delivering lectures on assorted topics. I have often thought that he must have been our first "Stand Up Comic".

The idea of writing really appealed to me since I had always written, mostly as a hobby. I was even published a couple of times in professional journals, but that was the extent of it. It seemed to me, though, that a life, like Clemens', spent in scholarly pursuit, writing books and regularly lecturing to audiences would be a wonderful way to spend my days and enjoying the process.

I was not able to find an actual job during my working years that encompassed these two elements (writing and public speaking), but I knew that in Retirement I would have the financial comfort and time availability to pursue this dream.

So, upon Retirement, I quickly signed up at my local community college for a book writing class, chose my first topic, and began the research and outlining that constitute the process origin. I finished the first book in a couple of years (just a bit each day) and I am now writing my second (you are reading it).

As for lecturing, I literally networked myself into a contract that a company held to provide workshops and presentations to federal government agencies. They sold their agency customers on the usefulness of my topic (emotional preparation for Retirement) and now I am booked to deliver lectures a couple of times a month. This pace is just perfect. I can satisfy my goal to talk to audiences two or three times a month and still have lots of time remaining to put words onto paper, as I am doing right now.

What about you? What will the ideal Retirement life look like for you?

Many people approach this question by starting with an assessment of their avocations (hobbies). What is it that you do in your life for which no one pays you? The likelihood is that, whatever that is, just might be a place to start in creating your "dream" for a Retirement activity and life.

I have learned firsthand of many examples of this.

There was a fellow that I met who was planning his Retirement from a medical research facility. He held a PhD in research as well as an MD, having been a practicing physician prior to switching to research.

He shared with me that, during the first week of his Retirement, he arranged for a construction company to come to his home and build a state-of-the-art greenhouse in his back yard.

The reasoning that he applied to arrive at this project was simple. He told me that during his 30+ year career that he had held several very high profile and high stress jobs. During those years, the way that he decompressed in the evenings and on weekends was to grow things. He loved the relaxation and enjoyment of planting things in his yard and at a local community garden. Watching what he had planted grow, and tending to them with diligence, was the way that he derived enormous satisfaction and felt refreshed in his soul, no matter the pressing issues at his job.

What a wonderful example of how to analyze one's joyful options and finding a way to expand these into productive actions during the years of Retirement. This speaks to who he is, at heart, and the process of growing plants and vegetables, now close to home, will be further relaxing and internally rewarding.

Oh, I am sure that he will do more things than just tend to his garden. But, this will be the "go to" activity that he knows from experience to be both relaxing and fulfilling.

One additional note. This gentleman further has shared with me, now that he is a couple of years into his Retirement, that he no longer identifies himself as "Doctor". Rather, when asked by new acquaintances about his profession, he refuses to say that he is "Retired". Instead, he introduces himself as a "botanist". And, certainly, that is what he is now.

It is important, I think, to be willing to reidentify ourselves once we have changed to a new path. For me, I no longer refer to myself as a Psychologist or a Human Resources professional because I am not engaged in that work anymore. But, when asked to identify my career identity, I say that either I am an "author" or a "philosopher". This is true in that I spend my time now enjoying life and writing and thinking about profound (for me) issues.

As another splendid example, I met a man who was within a few months of his Retirement date and he had a very interesting plan that involved his eldest son and an interesting relocation.

He shared that he and his eldest son had put some money together and purchased a business that they would own and run as equal partners. The plan recognized that a time would come when the Retired father would no longer be able to keep up in the running of the business and the father would "gift" his interests over time to his son, as the son took on a larger role in the running of the shop.

The business that they bought together is a fishing supplies store located right on a pier in Wilmington, North Carolina.

Why fishing supplies? The father told me that throughout his son's life the two of them had discovered a mutual passion for fishing. In fact, over the pre-teen and teenage years of the son, the two of them established a yearly tradition to go on a fishing trip, just the two of them, for about a week every Summer. The father said that it was on these trips that they got to know each other and learned to love each other for who they were.

Why Wilmington? Well, the father told me that he had attended both undergraduate and graduate schools at the University of North Carolina at Wilmington. He had met his wife there at that school and, after graduation, they married and relocated to the Washington, DC area from whence they both were raised.

Some years later, their son shopped several colleges and chose to attend his parents' alma mater. While there, the son met his wife, who was a native of that area, and they settled in the Wilmington suburbs upon graduation. They then raised their own family in that location.

During conversations about his parents' Retirement plans, he devised the plan to buy the fishing shop together and facilitate his parents' relocation and settling into life in the Wilmington community.

Here's the point. I believe that this was a wonderful life affirming plan that connected generations (several grandchildren by this time) and honored the father-son bond while providing an environment where the two would spend their days together surrounded by like-minded people (fishermen) and enjoying each other's company for the balance of the Retiree's days.

So, I ask: What might <u>your</u> life affirming plan consist of?

To get there, please give substantial self-reflective thought to who you are and who you want to be.

This will probably take some considerable exploration, so solicit the thoughts and ideas of those who know you the best. For many, that starts with one's life partner.

When there is a partner, remember that this plan includes them in equal measure. So, explore what will make you both the happiest and most satisfied. This will probably involve some negotiation with plenty of give and take. But, it is worth it to find the best goals that will last for many years of fulfillment.

Now for those who do not have a life partner, like me, I still know that it is possible to get help in the planning and dreaming for a Retirement plan.

I identified a small group of very close and trusted friends. These were people who had known me over many years and who had insight into what makes me who I am and from where I derive enjoyment. These friends were both a brainstorming group and a mirror against which I could try out ideas and garner feedback about the likelihood of finding joy in any given idea and life path.

This was immensely helpful to me in making good choices and avoiding the very human trait of kidding myself about various ideas.

And, here's an additional thought.

There is an exercise that I learned for how to think about the use of my time during Retirement, on days when I was neither traveling or otherwise employed. This was very helpful for me. I hope that it will be for you, as well.

Retirement Activity Plan
HOW TO UTILIZE TIME ONCE RETIRED

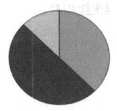

Take a blank piece of paper and draw a simple circle on it, large enough to fill most of the page. This circle is the beginning of a pie chart representing a day of Retirement.

The circle = a 24-hour period on any given day of Retirement.

Immediately, as in the sample above, you can eliminate (fill in) half of the circle. This is because you will be eating and sleeping close to half of the time.

But, what about the other 12 hours? How will you choose to utilize those? I've given you a few ideas below, but the things that you (or you and your partner) will choose to do that will constitute your waking hours will be unique and personal to you.

I will admit that I was shown this diagrammed thinking method when I first Retired and I had a tough time coming up with 12 hours of things to do. But, I continued to try and eventually filled in all the pie slices.

How will you use all 24 hours?

Relaxing?

Exercising?

Chores?

Meals?

Hobbies?

Volunteering?

What else?

And remember, it is just a "spitball" exercise meant to focus our thinking about these choices.

I believe that this is most helpful for life partners when each one starts with their own blank piece of paper and fills in a pie chart with their own thoughts. Best to not share as each goes about creating a chart. Then, when both feel that they are done, set the two charts side-by-side and look for areas of agreement and where there is divergence. Now, this is a great start to a conversation about activities that each feels strongly (or not so strongly) about and now there is a plan afoot.

And this is **BEST DONE in ADVANCE** of Retiring. In my experience, waiting until after the fact makes this a much more challenging task, for a variety of reasons.

CHAPTER 16

My Care Contract

(We'll do it MY way, thank you very much!)

ONCE I WAS told that I would require major, open-heart surgery, I began to wonder about the coming years of my life. If the operation would be successful (Ahem, it was ☺), I really started to question my preparations (or lack thereof) for growing older and sicker. I asked myself:

"Will my family know what I want done at the end of my life???"

"Do they know what kind of care and living arrangements I will want as I age??"

"What can I do to ensure that my family will know what to do at every stage of my life and death, particularly after I'm no longer able to speak for myself?"

The unfortunate truth was that I had never addressed these issues with any of my family members.

Oh, I joked about my death as a cause for spectacular galas and celebrations all around. And, I remember several times when the topic of disposal of my remains came up, I made cringe-worthy jokes about the absurdity of holding onto rotting flesh.

I told my family members who would listen that I certainly was to be cremated. And that this was to be done only after 100% of my reusable organs have been harvested.

I'm not sure why it should even be necessary to add the harvesting instructions. I just can't imagine a reason why ANYONE would NOT want to do this. Really. It's not as though we need them when we're dead.

I am amused when I think about this for me, though. At the rate that I am using up this wonderful body of mine, I would be surprised if any part of me will still be useful to anyone. Maybe my eyelids? Well, anything that has served me well should be removed and given to anyone who can use the thing.

And, when they asked about what to do with my ashes, I boldly told them, "Oh, a Burial at Sea" is the thing for me.

Then I would pantomime that I was holding a jar in one hand and pouring portions downwards. And then with my other hand I made the motion of pushing down the lever on a toilet chamber while I smiled broadly and said, "Oh, it all goes to the same place and, trust me, I really won't care at that point" (Big smiles from me. Uncertain grins from the family.).

Well, I realized that this was woefully insufficient as a preparation for them to know and follow my post-mortem wishes.

And, what about my pre-mortem wishes?

My family knew that, as a Veteran, I am entitled to some level of care at a VA facility when I need long term care. But, they certainly didn't know how to make that happen for me. And, whose fault is that?

Well, I have always claimed to be the master of my own destiny.

So, I jumped right in and started writing. At first, I intended the document to be a letter to my family members. But somewhere along the way, I changed the format and title of the document and it became a "contract" that I would sign, as well as both my brother and my sister, as well as my sons. This way, I was surer that the holder of my Health Power of Attorney would be held to scrutiny by my family members. Everyone will know what I want and how I want it. I called this document my **"Care Contract"** and all my family members have a copy. Hopefully, by all having signed copies of this document, they will keep each other honest and on point with my wishes, not their fallible memories of my wishes many years later.

I suspect that you may be thinking, "Isn't this document duplicating the Advanced Directive or Living Will (different names of this document in different states)?"

Well, I don't believe so. The Living Will is a document that is addressed to our health care providers. Much of what is in the Living Will reflects my broader instructions in my **Care Contract**. I have made sure that they are not contradictory and I feel very confident now that my wishes will be acknowledged and followed by all who are involved with my care as time goes along.

At this point, I would like to advocate in the strongest possible terms for all my fellow Seniors to consider and adopt such a document themselves.

Let me repeat my reasoning from above, it's that important. I have noticed that many of my fellow seniors are lucky enough to live nice long lives, as, so far, can be said of me. But, for so many, because they avoid or simply fail to have the conversation with their family, as they age, families make decisions about the elder's care based on their own common sense. It's as if so many seniors just sit there, aging in place, experiencing the common frailties and illnesses of aging. And all the while, the senior is just waiting to see what everyone else is going to do for them.

Well, I decided some time ago that this is not for me.

I decided that my family members all need to know what my wishes and preferences are as I age and my needs change. Yes, I want them to know who I want to be cared for, based on MY preferences and values, not on THEIRS. This is, after all, about me, not them.

I would note, too, the importance of having thought all of this through while in my early sixties while I was still somewhat compos mentis and able to discern and clearly communicate my wishes. We all know that, later in life, memory and cognition fade. I want to be realistic about this coming event and take care of the most critical things that I'll need my sharpest self to satisfactorily complete.

Oh, and I rejected the option to simply have a formal or informal talk with my key family members to tell them all that is contained in my **Care Contract**. The reason for feeling the need to commit all of this to writing is quite simple.

In the years that I have enjoyed life on this planet, I have noticed that when families rely on their memories regarding vital details, they so often are dim on the details and even contradictory in their recollections.

I'm sure that you have noticed this, as well. Yes, memories fade over time, but the written word does not. In fact, in the immortal words of one of my graduate school Psychology professors, "*When there is Trauma... There will be Drama...*" And, boy have I seen this to be the case. Haven't you?

At a time when families are stressed due to illness or misfortune of a loved one, arguments about what to do for the ailing one are regular and, often, vehement. Yes, family members will correct each other, imposing a different memory of what the ailing family wanted to be done for them. Interestingly, I have seen just this scenario lead to years of disharmony and, even, distancing of siblings and others over faulty memories.

Well, therefore, I believed it necessary to commit my wishes to writing in the clearest language that I could summon.

Not only that, I asked each of my closest relatives (both sons, and my closest brother and sister) to sign the five copies of the document and each has a copy signed by all others. This may (just may) safeguard my wishes by all key parties knowing what I have wanted and keeping each other honest in the process.

Again, I want to be cared for MY way, not someone else's.

And, you might ask if this written document in any way guarantees that I'll live out the remaining stages of my life, cared for in the ways that I've indicated... Well, I'm realistic enough to recognize that there are NO guarantees in life. Anything can happen. But, I feel as though it has been important to let my family know my wishes – well in advance of the need for interventions.

So, here's the stripped-down version of my **Care Contract**. I have, of course, redacted much of the instructional parts because that's a bit personal and I am not advocating for anyone to make the same choices, necessarily, that I have made. But there's enough here, I think, for you to get the gist and, hopefully, create your own contract/instructions for your benefit (and your family's).

Care Contract for Michael Townshend

Dated:

Items:

A. Where I will live

Levels of Care and the Observable Triggers and Measures

When I require help, here's how to pay for it _____

B. When I can no longer live alone – Assisted Living

Observable Triggers and Measurements:

Here are 9 things to consider in assessing if I need Assisted Living

Here's what to look for

1. Big-picture signs it might be time for me to get assisted living

Keep the big red flags in mind. Certain situations make it more obvious that it's wise to start thinking about alternate living arrangements.

Look for:

Recent accidents or close calls.

Did I take a <u>fall</u>, have a medical scare, or get in a fender bender (or worse)? Who responded and how long did it take? Accidents do happen, but as I get older, the odds rise of them happening again.

A slow recovery.

How did I weather the most recent illness (for example, a flu or bad cold)? Was I able and willing to seek medical care when needed?

A chronic health condition that's worsening.

Progressive problems such as COPD, dementia, and congestive heart failure can decline gradually or precipitously, but either way, their presence means I will increasingly need help.

Increasing difficulty managing the activities of daily living (ADLs) and instrumental activities of daily living (IADLs).

<u>ADLs and IADLs</u> are the skills needed to live independently -- dressing, shopping, cooking, doing laundry, managing medications, and so on. Difficulties with ADLs and IADLs can sometimes be remedied by bringing in more <u>in-home help</u>. Consider that first, of course.

2. Up-close signs it might be time for assisted living

Occasionally, give me a big hug. Clues aren't always visible from a distance; especially when you don't see me every day, you might learn more through touch.

Look for:

Noticeable weight loss.

Do I appear thinner? Are clothes loose, or have I added notches to my belt?

Many conditions, from <u>depression</u> to <u>cancer</u>, can cause weight loss. If I am having trouble getting out to shop or remembering how to cook (or to eat) these can explain loss of weight; check the fridge and watch meal-prep skills.

Seeming frailer.

• Do you feel anything "different" about my strength and stature when you hug?

- Can I rise easily from a chair?
- Do I seem unsteady or unable to balance?

Compare these observations to the last time we were together.

Noticeable weight gain.

Common causes include an injury slowing me down, diabetes, and dementia (when I don't remember eating, I indulge in meals and snacks all day long). If I'm having money troubles I may choose fewer fresh foods and more packaged goods or dried pasta and bread.

Body odor.

A close hug can also reveal changes in personal hygiene habits. Causes range from memory trouble to depression to other physical ailments.

Changes in appearance.

- Does my hair look all right?
- Are clothes clean?
- You've known my preference for crisply ironed shirts, but if I'm more often in a stained sweatshirt or the like, it may be because I lack the dexterity for buttons or may have lost the strength for managing an ironing board and iron.

- Notice if I'm often forgetting to shave (or forgetting <u>how</u> to shave).

3. Social signs it might be time for assisted living

Think realistically about my social connections. Social circles tend to shrink with age, which can have health and safety implications.

Look for:

Signs of active friendships.

- Do I still get together for lunches or outings with friends or visits with neighbors, or participate in religious activities or other group events?
- Do I talk about others?
- Do I keep a calendar of appointments?

NOTE: My research has revealed that a lack of companionship is associated with depression and heart problems in older adults. If friends have died or moved away, moving to a place where other people are around could be lifesaving.

Signs that I have cut back on activities and interests.

- Is a hobby area abandoned?
- Has a club membership been given up?
- A library card gone unused?

NOTE: There are many reasons people cut back, but dropping out of everything and showing interest in almost nothing is a red flag for <u>depression</u>.

Days spent without leaving the house.

This will happen naturally once I can <u>no longer drive</u> or I become fearful of taking public transportation alone.

NOTE: When the time comes for assisted living I may well fear being "locked away" in a retirement home. But please remind me that these facilities offer regular outings that may keep me more mobile and active, not less.

Is there someone who checks in with me on a regular basis?

If this is not convenient for anyone in the family or a close friend of mine, I should consider a <u>home-safety alarm system</u>, a personal alarm system, or a daily calling service? Please explore these options with me.

A plan for a worst-case scenario.

If there's a fire, earthquake, flood, or other disaster, is someone on standby to assist? Does everyone understand the plan?

4. Money signs it might be time for assisted living

Rifle through my mail. Mail can offer an often-overlooked clue to how I am managing money, a common early warning sign of cognitive trouble.

Look for:

Snowdrifts of mail in various places.

Finding lots of mail scattered around raises concern about how I am managing bills, insurance, and other matters. (Piles of mail are also a potential tripping hazard.)

Unopened personal mail.

Everybody skips junk mail, but few of us can ignore a good old-fashioned, hand-addressed letter. When I let personal mail just sit unopened, something is up with me.

Accumulated emails.

Check my email cache a couple of times a year. When I am failing to even open emails, I'm showing you that I'm very distracted, at the very least.

Unopened bills.

This can indicate that I am having difficulty managing finances -- one of the most common first signs of dementia, by the way.

Letters from banks, creditors, or insurers.

Routine business letters aren't worrisome. But it's alarming if correspondence is referring to overdue payments, overdrawn balances, recent accidents, or other concerning events. Bring these to my attention without a sense of judgment and try to talk to me about these with a sense of concern and offering to help me. I'll respond much more positively to adult-adult conversations. Please don't assume that I need to be addressed in a childlike or disrespectful manner.

Thankyou messages from charities.

Older adults are often vulnerable to scammers. Even though I have always been fiscally prudent, I will be as vulnerable as anyone else and this will indicate that I am having trouble with thinking skills (a common sign of Alzheimer's disease). Some charities hit up givers over and over, and I may not remember donating the first time.

Lots of crisp, unread magazines.

It happens to many older folks that they unknowingly have repeat-renewal subscriptions that they don't need. If this seems to be the case for me, please show me the evidence and offer to help cancel unwanted subscriptions and duplications.

5. Kitchen signs it might be time for assisted living

Go through the kitchen, from fridge to cupboards to oven. Because I'll be spending so much time in this room, you can learn a lot.

Look for:

Stale or expired foods.

We all buy more than we need. Look for signs that food is not only old but that this is unnoticed -- mold, sour milk that's still used, or expiration dates well past due, for example. You know me. I have always been a stickler for expiration dates. We've probably laughed about this together many times over the years. If this changes in my behavior – that's a huge flag.

Multiples of the same item.

Ten bottles of ketchup? More cereal than can be eaten in a year? Multiples will likely reveal that I can't remember from one store trip to the next what's in stock at home. Again, a Red Flag as you know how meticulous I've been in the years that you've known me.

A freezer full of TV dinners.

I've always kept a few on hand for convenience sake, but frozen dinners as a sole source of nutrition tends to make an unhealthy diet. If there's not much fresh food in the house (because it's too hard to for me to procure or cook),

I might be ready to have help with meal prep or delivery services.

Broken appliances.

Check them all: microwave, coffeemaker, toaster, washer, and dryer -- any device you know I use (or used to use) routinely.

Signs of fire. <u>This is a deadly serious sign to observe</u>.

- Are stove knobs charred?
- Pot and pan bottoms singed badly (or thrown out)?
- Do any potholders have burned edges?
- Also look for a discharged fire extinguisher, smoke detectors that have been disassembled, or boxes of baking soda near the stove.
- Accidents happen; ask for the story behind what you see. <u>Accidental fires are a common home danger for older adults.</u>

Increased use of takeout or simpler cooking.

A change in my physical or mental abilities might explain a downshift to simpler recipes or food choices.

6. Around-the-house signs it might be time for assisted living

Look around my home. Sometimes the most obvious sign is hard to see because we become so used to it.

Look for:

Lots of clutter.

An inability to throw anything away may be a sign of a neurological or physical issue. This will be a worrisome sign for me because I have tended to be chronically neat and keep a clean house/living space. Papers or books all over the floor represent a tripping hazard. Inordinate layers of dust will be harmful to my sinuses as I age.

Signs of lax housekeeping.

Spills that haven't been cleaned up are a common sign of dementia – it will indicate that I lack the follow-through to tidy. Keep an eye out for cobwebs, bathroom mold, thick dust, or other signs of slackness. Physical limitations can mean I need housekeeping help or a living situation where this is taken care of by him or her.

Bathroom grime and clutter.

A common scenario: If I try to tidy up living areas but overlook the bathroom. Or the guest bath is clean, but not the one that I use all the time (the one off my bedroom, for example). Here you may see a truer picture of how I am keeping up.

7. Home-maintenance signs it might be time for assisted living

Walk around the yard. Yard maintenance -- or lack of it -- can yield clues that I'm not faring as well at home alone anymore.

Look for:

Signs of neglect.

Look for discolored siding or ceilings that might indicate a leak, gutters choked with leaves, broken windows or fences, dirty windows.

Newspapers in the bushes.

Are papers being delivered but ignored? Sometimes I'll pick up those I can see on my driveway but not those that go off into the yard.

Mail piled up in the mailbox.

Go out and check -- it's an indication that I'm no longer retrieving it regularly.

8. Get help looking for signs it might be time for assisted living

Get the input of others who know me well to collect a fuller picture of reality. Gently probing about what others think isn't nosy; you're being loving, concerned, and proactive.

Look for:

Input from those in my close circle.

Talk to old friends and close relatives to get their sense of how I am faring. Listen for stories that hint that I don't get out much ("He doesn't come over anymore." "He quit book club."). Pay attention to comments that indicate that my closest friends and neighbors have ongoing concerns ("Has he had that heart test yet?" "We were worried the day the ambulance came.").

Medical insight.

I have given the appropriate permission for my primary care doctor to discuss your concerns about my safety at home -- or my doctor may be able to alleviate those concerns or suggest where to get a home assessment. I have executed an overall permission, compliant with the HIPPA rules, for my closest family members to be able to speak freely with my primary care physician.

A second opinion.

You may want to engage a social worker or professional geriatric care manager to visit my home and do an informal evaluation.

While I may initially resist the notion of a "total stranger" checking on me, try pitching it as a professional (and neutral) second opinion, or ask the doctor to "prescribe" it. I may, at that point, be willing to share doubts or vulnerabilities with a sympathetic, experienced stranger that I might be loath to admit to my own children or family.

9. Caregivers' signs it might be time for assisted living

Finally, I realize that some of the information you collect is intangible -- it is about feelings and emotions, and the stress levels of everyone involved.

Look for:

How <u>you</u>'re doing.

While this decision to remain in my home is not primarily about you -- my son, daughter-in-Law, grandchild, and caregiver -- your own exhaustion can be a good gauge of a decline in my ability to care for myself. Keeping me at home can require lots of hands-on support or care coordination, and this is time-consuming. If my need for care is just plain <u>wearing you out</u>, or if other family and friends are feeling the collective strain of your caregiving activities, these are major signs that it's time to start looking at other options. I instruct you now to strongly consider a move for me and you should show me this section of this Care Contract to remind me that this was my thinking at the time that I wrote this document.

My emotional state.

- Safety is crucial, of course, but so is emotional well-being. If while living alone I am riddled with anxieties or increasingly lonely, then that may tip the scales toward a move not solely based on health and safety reasons.
- If I have a full life, a close neighborhood and community connections, and seem to be thriving, it's worth exploring as many in-home care options as possible before raising stress levels by pressing a move from my beloved home.
- If, on the other hand, I am showing signs that living alone is a strain, it may be time for a talk. Broach the subject of where to live in a neutral way and you may find that I harbor the same fears for current and future safety and security that you do. Find out what I fear most about moving and about staying before launching into your own worries and what you think ought to be done.

C. End my Driving

Observable Triggers and Measurements: (here's what you are to see that indicates that I should no longer drive an automobile [or whatever we're driving around in then])

Driving behaviors triggering intervention:

- Difficulty merging into traffic or staying in lane
- Abrupt lane changes
- Increased aggressiveness or irritation while driving
- Speeding or going too slow for road conditions
- More than two fender benders or unexplained dents on the car, garage, or mailbox during a calendar year
- More than two Warnings or Traffic tickets within a calendar year
- Difficulty turning my head or moving my foot from the gas pedal to the brake
- Getting lost in familiar surroundings more than once in a calendar year
- Using a "co-pilot" to direct driving

SOURCES: *The Washington Post*; AARP; National Highway Traffic Safety Administration; The Hartford; AAA Foundation for Safety

When you see that I am doing the above, here's what you are to do:

The possessor of my Power-of-Attorney is to:

1. Come to my home (bring anyone else you would like to be there, but I am determined that you should not need "Backup"
2. Show me this document, reminding me that this is MY instruction as to what I will do
3. Ask for and receive my car keys
4. Sell my car (the cash is to be returned to my cash account)
5. **From this date forward, I will find alternative means of transportation** (this is an instruction to

my older self, so show it to me in writing and that my signature is found at the bottom of this page).

D. When I am sick

Measures to be taken – under what circumstances –Also, see Advance Directive/Living Will

1. What level of medical care I will have
2. Who I would like to visit me (NOT mandatory – EVER)
3. When to keep me alive – let's give it a while to see if I come back
4. When to let me die – here's what you must see to be happening – then, **you have my permission to terminate my life** – keep smiling, kiddo, it's the way I want it, and this is about me, not you

E. When I Die

1. What <u>funeral arrangements</u>
2. <u>Memorial</u> details
3. <u>Harvesting of my organs</u> (I bequeath 100% of what's needed and still working, and I've already made these arrangements with the State of Maryland – give my driver's license and donor card to the hospice, they'll know what to do)
4. <u>Disposal of my body</u> (I bequeath this tub for the use of medical education where it can be of assistance

in any way at all – probably just a good laugh, but that's worth quite a lot in my book, and, again, I've already made these arrangements with the State of Maryland – look in my wallet and give the card that you'll find in there to the hospice and they will know what to do)

Attached:

Advance Directive/Living Will
Last Will and Testament
A detailed listing of all Assets and Debts
Where to find all financial papers (A Road Map)

Note: A copy of this document outline can be easily accessed on my website: www.MyBestDayIsToday.com by going to the site and clicking on the page titled, "Books and Materials". On that page, you will find a link titled, "Free Materials". Click on that link and two links drop down, "Financial Road Map" and "Care Contract". When you click on either of these links the material will automatically download onto your computer, free of charge. Your computer will create a "pop up" asking where you would like to store the document(s). And you will now have a usable copy of each document to use as you wish.

CHAPTER 17

Relationships During Retirement

WELL, HERE'S A news flash: Relationships change, once we are Retired.

Even our significant partnership relationship will change and we need to be sure that we are prepared to manage the new reality. Well, sure. If nothing else, the amount of "face time" that we encounter will change daily. In many cases, we have been in each other's company mostly from the time we returned from work in an evening until the time we leave the next morning. Weekends, of course, have often contained more time together, but we have usually planned outings and visits for those days.

So, the new reality, once Retired, will normally replicate the weekends – only that will be every day of the week.

Here's my bottom line:

- Talk with your spouse/partner and your family **before** your Retirement date
- Explore the options for your individual and partnered life ahead
- What does each of you want?
- What are your dreams?
- Tell each other with honesty about your desires and needs – **Please Don't ASSUME**
- Make decisions about how to spend your time in Retirement – both individually and collectively
- Prior to Retirement, take concrete steps to start Retirement activities and plans. For example: if you and your significant partner decide to travel a little, or a lot, research the first trip in advance of Retirement. Even pay for the trip in advance. This is a way to bridge the "dreams" of activities and enter the "reality" of them.
- If one of you would like to work after Retiring, research possible full or part time jobs and, even, set up such a job with a start date after Retirement. Again, this moves you from "theory" to "reality" on this topic. Plus, you will have a chance to test your assumptions about the existence of jobs that would fit your vision.

Has one spouse been at home?

Sometimes, upon Retirement, a stay-at-home spouse/ partner will be just as eager to start the Retirement journey as the Retiree. But, be careful. There are potential road hazards ahead.

I recommend as much discussion and planning in advance of the Retirement date as possible. The items to be discussed are many, but the most critical is to share with each other our vision of what Retired life will be like. Get as much of each other's "wish list" on the table as possible and talk your way through the list to find points of agreement and negotiate where your visions may conflict.

This is essential to do. Here is a scenario that I have heard on several occasions from partners, post Retirement, and they are eerily similar when shared with me.

The working spouse Retires. There is great fanfare at the office prior to the last day and some of the social events include the partner, so both seem to be on the same page.

And then, just a few weeks later, the Retiree is sitting on the couch reading the daily newspaper when the at-home partner enters and sits across the room wearing a stone-cold look on his or her face.

Shortly, the Retiree notices the clearly angry presence and puts down the paper asking, "What's wrong, Dear?"

The reply, "So here you sit. Just like every day so far since you Retired. I would just like to know. Is this IT? Is this your "Plan"?

Retiree, "Honey, what's the real problem? We discussed our Retirement years, didn't we? Why is my sitting here such a surprise?"

Spouse/partner, "You said that you had many things that you wanted to do. I figured that the first couple of weeks would be spent just getting your bearings and that you would start your Retirement activities by now."

Retiree, "Well what's wrong with me being here at the house a lot? I am, after all, retired now and this is where I am most comfortable."

Spouse/partner, "The problem is that this is MY house. It has been my house for all the years of our marriage, certainly from the early hours every day when you prepared and left for work. And it remained MY house until you returned each evening, at least during the week. You see, I have become used to working around the house, as I see fit. I prepare meals when I feel hungry and I go about chores and socialize with my friends when I feel like it. And, now you are here.

You seem to assume that I am here to wait on you hand and foot. At lunch time, for example, you keep asking me what I will be preparing. Really? What's wrong with your hands and head? Why can't you prepare lunch for us? Why do you assume that this is my job?"

Retiree, "I'm sorry, dear. Maybe we should have talked about this before I Retired. My bad."

Well, dear reader, you see where this very typical clash has its origins and why it escalates into a very bruising exchange between two partners who should both be enjoying the Retirement Years.

So, knowing that this is just one of a variety of clashes that is destined to take place, I advise all couples to sit down BEFORE Retirement and talk to each other about what each will expect – what Retirement looks like to each. Talking about this in advance of Retirement will not avoid all confrontations, but it will set a frame work for being able to openly share feelings during the Retirement Years.

Has one spouse done certain chores?

This is quite often the case. Along the years of working together as a couple, most often the chores of daily living (lawn care, dry cleaning runs, house cleaning, clothes washing, household repairs, and the like) have been split up for a variety of reasons.

My advice is, though, BEFORE Retirement, have a conversation where you write out all the various chores that are necessary. Put all those chores "on the table". Decide anew which of us will tend to which chores, once Retirement commences.

Don't be surprised if your partner volunteers for a chore or two that you have hereto for owned. That's not unusual.

I met a couple at the 55+ condominium where I used to live where the husband, who had never lifted a finger in the kitchen (said that he "couldn't boil water") during the years of their marriage, asked to learn how and take over the cooking for the couple.

This came as a shock to the wife, but, being a very smart lady, she stepped backwards out of the kitchen and turned it over to him.

He told me that at first, he assumed that if he just read all the cook books in the kitchen that he would surely be able to cook deliciously (typical Retired Engineer). Her response was, "OK. If you think it is that easy. I'll be out here in the sun room reading every day. Let me know any questions you encounter".

Well, eventually, he got the hang of it – after about a year of pitiful tasting meals. He even took cooking classes at the local community college. And, he even spent a week in New York learning pastry baking at the Cordon Bleau Chef's school.

My point is, by being open to each other's possibilities and not holding on to past duties as though they are cast in stone, an enjoyable time is more likely for both.

Are we retiring together (at the same time)?

I have some advice for couples who have both been working for years and who are both planning a Retirement (Yippee! 2 incomes during Retirement – Great!). This scenario is quite promising of many happy years to come.

But, be careful!

Did you know that when two people plan to Retire, it is rare (it happens, but…) that the eligibility dates will coincide? And, unless some planning is done carefully, there is a mine field to be avoided.

So, the hurdle here is navigating the time in between the two Retirements.

If the amount of time from the first Retirement until the second is one year or less, there seems to be only minor irritations that will occur. Nothing that can't smooth over with ease. (I think that this is because you can both see the light at the end of the tunnel.) It is, after all, a brief period.

However, the amount of time difference can also be much longer. Yes. Especially if you married younger or older – here comes the down side. There can be years of difference for some couples and the longer the difference, the higher the likelihood of conflict if the groundwork has not been clearly laid.

Yet, here's a remedy. Talk and plan the time in between. And, here's the most helpful topic to create the atmosphere for success. Talk openly and honestly about "Expectations". For many, it's just that simple.

What I mean is, sit together (probably several times) and imagine the time after which the first partner Retires and the point at which the second partner can do so.

Most importantly, <u>ask each other to express</u>: what will we expect of each other during that time?

Who will see to what chores?

Once the first partner is Retired, what will the continuing worker expect the Retiree to do around the house or other things for the sake of both?

Conversely, what will the first Retiree expect of the continuing worker?

Do the shopping on the way home?

Do nothing domestic at all?

Arise in the morning very quietly so that I can continue to sleep? (How will that feel?)

Let's agree to have breakfast together each day when practical?

And, so forth.

To omit this planning process runs the risk of grave and hurtful experiences that will seem trivial to an outside observer but have the potential to create a deep divide between two people who otherwise love each other.

This is advice given from the experience of many couples who have navigated the same previously unforeseen issues. Many have ended up in couples or marriage counseling. In those counseling sessions, the therapist leads the couple to the topic of "Expectations" every time. Now, address this in advance and, hopefully, pave the way for a wonderful experience.

Is our "Retirement Activity Plan" clear and are both in agreement?

I have advised throughout this section of this book that it is critical to have a **Retirement Plan** if we would prefer a joy filled set of years, rather than a monotonous repeat each day of the day before.

To arrive at a workable and fun life there are several considerations.

- First, create a Dream for the activity of the final leg of our life journey
- Then, refine the Dream into an actionable plan
- Be sure to create a Daily Plan
- And, finally, imagine a Back Up Plan for when the initial Plans cease to be realistic

Create a Dream

Here is a fanciful but extremely helpful step in preparing one's Retirement Plan.

I created my plan based on the life of one of my literary heroes, Mark Twain (Samuel Clemmons). Twain lived his life writing books and articles for newspapers, as well as delivering lectures across America and the world. I have often said that I think that he was the first "Stand Up Comic", though many would argue that honor belongs to William Shakespeare. But, no matter.

I was really taken with the way that he could live his life and make a sufficient income to live very well – all without the benefit of a regular job. And, I thought that I would just love to spend my life doing the same.

After all, I always enjoyed writing. It was a hobby of mine throughout my life. I was published with a couple of articles in professional journals, but nothing else.

Also, the most fun and interesting part of any job that I have held was the opportunity to deliver speeches in front of audiences, whether teaching a course or leading a workshop.

But, in the end, I was never able to find an actual job that would compensate me reasonably doing just those two things.

So, when I started thinking about my Retirement, somewhere in my 50's, I thought that this would be the time in my life when I would finally be able to afford to live the life that most interested me. I decided that spending my Retired days writing books and, perhaps, plays and short stories, and finding speaking engagements would make for a truly rewarding and interesting life. This became my dream.

Now the question for you, dear reader, is: <u>What will your dream be</u>?

What are your hobbies that you might turn into a semi-full time activity?

Let me give you a couple of examples.

I met a fellow who was a senior scientist at National Institutes of Health who was about to Retire after 35+ years of service. He told me that in anticipation of his Retirement, he had engaged a construction company to come to his home and build, in his back yard, a state-of-the-art greenhouse.

Here's why.

He told me that throughout his career, he had held highly responsible and stress-filled jobs. The way that he found to decompress from the stress of these jobs was to grow plants, vegetables, flowers, and small bonsai trees. Having his fingers in the soil, he told me, was a wonderful relief that would take his mind off the challenges of his career and relax him immensely.

Today, a couple of years after Retirement, he now refers to himself as a "Botanist" because of how he spends the bulk of his Retired time.

Another fellow that I met from the Environmental Protection Agency was scheduled to Retire just a few months after we met. He shared with me that his Retirement Plan included relocating from Washington, DC to Wilmington, NC. His adult son already lived in the Wilmington suburbs and this gentleman and his son had put some money together and bought a business on the waterfront of Wilmington that they would own and operated together.

Here's why.

The man from EPA had gone to both undergraduate and graduate schools at the University of North Carolina in Wilmington many years ago. He had, in fact, met his wife there but relocated to take the job with the EPA.

Some years later, their son also attended the University of North Carolina – Wilmington, met his wife there and opted to stay in Wilmington to raise their family.

Interestingly, the Retiring gentleman told me that he and his son shared a passion for fishing. In fact, they had established a ritual where for every year of his son's life, they had gone together on a one week trip, just the two of them, to enjoy fishing. He told me that on these trips is where he and his son got to really know each other and that they cherished the trips and constant banter about fishing throughout the years.

So, what kind of business did they buy? A fishing supply business. And, this sounded so appropriate to me since they will now be surrounded by customers who are like-minded fishermen and women. Throughout the balance of the Retiree's years, he will be able to fish often with his son and turn over the business when he is no longer able to contribute to its running. And, it's important to note that he will be near his grandchildren and daughter-in-law. Great Plan!

Michael Townshend

Refine the Dream

Once a dream is in vision, the next step is to refine that dream. This is the process of adding meat to the bones.

For me, I knew that it was not enough to just decide to write and speak publicly. I put some time into describing the kinds of things to do that would accomplish the dream. And, I committed my thoughts to paper and then tested them.

First, I researched the kinds of writing projects that are possible and learned how others had gone about the dream of becoming a writer and a speaker. I found volumes written on these topics.

So, I read and studied these methods to uncover the way forward for me in both areas. I wrote down my thoughts and discoveries about these topics and paths forward.

Then, and this is critical, I knew that to control myself from delusion, I needed to pass these ideas in front of others who care about me and know me very well. Usually, people in a partnership relationship have a built-in reviewer in the person of their partner. But, I did not have someone with whom I was then partnered, so I thought about the knowledgeable friendships that I am so fortunate to have.

322

I called these folks (Just 3 or 4) my "kitchen cabinet". I sent my written thoughts to them and, after a few weeks, invited them to a series of brunches asking for their feedback.

There was universal support for my dream, but conflicting ideas about my execution plan. This was great. I took all their feedback to heart. They know me in a depth that is enormously helpful for me.

Of course, I sorted through the ideas and chose, tested, and settled upon a way forward based on the coupling of the feedback and my own personal life compass.

Today, as I pointed out above, I am living my dream. And, I don't mind saying that I am roundly enjoying every day of my life.

Create a Daily Plan

Now, this part of Retirement planning is about thinking through how we will spend our time on a day-to-day basis. This would be, of course, on days when we are not traveling or otherwise engaged with a major project or activity.

Retirement Activity Plan

HOW TO UTILIZE TIME ONCE RETIRED

The circle = a 24-hour period. How will you use all 24 hours? How much relaxing? Exercising? Chores? Meals? Hobbies? Volunteering?

What else?

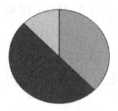

SLEEPING = 6 to 9 hours +
EATING = 2 to 3 hours

So, to make this exercise useful, please do the following.

Take a blank piece of paper (if you have a partner in life, each should take a blank piece of paper, not showing their ideas to the other until done. Only then, compare the two charts and discuss similarities and differences.)

This circle that you have drawn is the beginning of a Pie Chart representing 24 hours of any day of Retirement.

As the sample indicates, you can eliminate about half of the circle right away, as we will utilize about half of our normal daily time eating and sleeping.

But the remaining 12 hours? How will you use your time during those waking hours? I gave a few ideas above, but think carefully about your use of time when it's all your choosing and capture the activities that will add up to 12 hours. This was not easy for me when I first tried it. But I am glad that I stuck with it and I found that I was more confident than I had thought about how I would spend the days of my Retired life.

Imagine a Back Up Plan

I want to emphasize that the first "dream" that we create will, if implemented in a thoughtful way, launch us into years of enjoyment of our Retirement journey. I suggest that all of us sit back periodically during our journey and appreciate where we came from to get here and how much fun we experience daily. (more about Appreciation in the next chapter)

But, while all this fun will engulf our days and render such good feelings, we also need to be realistic about this truth. Our Retirement journey will have phases of change that can be predicted and counted on. These phases will allow us more and more physical and cognitive limits on what we are able to do with comfort.

Therefore, several back up plans are important to keep "at the ready".

The phases to which I refer are these:

- ❖ We will lose stamina and physical ability over time
- ❖ We will experience lessening of memory and cognitive capabilities
- ❖ We will lose others in our inner circle to death
- ❖ We will experience periods of hospitalization and recovery from the predictable health debilities
- ❖ Others in our family and inner circle may have needs that will cause us to devote time, energy, and, perhaps, financial support
- ❖ And so, the list goes.

Let me share a sad example.

During the years that I lived in a Senior Community just outside of Washington, DC, I met quite a variety of older folks who were experiencing varying levels of their Retirement Plans.

One fellow that I met in the condo building where we both lived showed me the value of a back up to our Retirement Plan.

This fellow had been Retired for over 15 years when we met. For several years, he seemed to be alert and fully engaged in his life - always positive and responsive to social engagement, as best I could tell at a distance.

And then, very suddenly, he seemed to change for the worse.

I noticed him sitting in the lobby of our building every single day when I would enter from the near-by garage.

He would look up from his seat on a couch when each neighbor entered the lobby, usually to fetch our mail. His face revealed a deep sadness that I had not seen before. And this look, with his presence in the lobby, became predictable and more and more painful to see.

So, I sat with him on that couch one afternoon and asked him if he was alright.

He told me that he was sitting in the lobby because his apartment had become too depressing.

He shared with me that upon his Retirement, he learned of a degenerative illness that his wife would live with for some years. She told him that she wanted to stay at home with him in their apartment for as long as possible. He told her that his life's mission would be to become her care giver allowing her to stay at home just a long as possible.

Caring for his ill wife became his Retirement Plan. He took classes in how to best care for her and bought the equipment needed to stay at home (hospital bed, oxygen equipment, and the like). This had given him purpose and pleasure (a labor of love) and that seemed to be all that he required over the next decade and a half.

However, eventually she died at home and not only was the hospital equipment removed from the apartment, his purposeful Retirement Plan was no longer workable.

As we talked that afternoon, he told me that even though he knew that she would die at some point, he did not create a backup plan to sustain his remaining years. He felt lost, totally alone, and without purpose. He even said to me, "I just don't know why I should get up each morning. I can't think of a good reason..."

I invited him to my apartment for several visits and conversation over coffee.

During these talks, we kicked around many ideas about what he might do as a new Retirement Plan.

He had Retired but he was still a lawyer and a member-emeritus of the State Bar. He seemed to have a strong feeling for and closeness to so many of our fellow seniors who were experiencing the same kinds of disconnect that he felt, some much worse. So many of these folks lived in our very senior community.

At my suggestion, he renewed his law license and set up a very part time practice at the community's activity center where he offered advice (nearly for free) to other seniors regarding their estates, wills, trusts, and the like.

He also started and led small group support meetings for seniors who had lost their life partner. This became a very popular activity at the senior center and he told me that he took immense joy from the process.

Well, this is the process of establishing a backup plan that I am encouraging here.

For myself, I recognize that my health will someday limit my mobility and my memory will be challenged. This is based on the known ailments that have been diagnosed and are, by nature, degenerative.

So, I have researched and put into writing several backup plans that I will be able to accomplish at each stage.

First, I have volunteered to go to the local Veterans Center in my town where I will work with young Vets who are preparing for the job market. I will review their resumes and help them prepare to interview in our job market. I spent nearly 40 years in Human Resources functions, so, who better.

I also walked the route from the front of the Veterans Center entrance to the rooms where I will donate my time. I have measured for accessibility once I am in a wheel chair or mobility scooter. Of course, having reviewed the mobility access was already considered by the Center staff for the sake of the Veteran clients.

I also met with the local police department to establish the rules and permissions to make my way to the Center in my scooter where sidewalks are non-existent.

As for my memory challenge, yet to come, I have put labels on each of my kitchen cabinets to indicate what glasses, plates, pots, and pans are in each. Someday I know that I won't remember these things. Now I am ready.

Also, I have used the label maker to affix to the counters of my bathroom sink top. These spell out the different medications that are to be taken at specific times and intervals. Again, I can take my medications now with relative ease, but I know that degeneration of cognition is coming and I want to be prepared.

All of this will allow me to live on my own for many more years and that is my Retirement Plan.

I spend my days now writing at my computer (what fun!), as right now is the case. And, a few of times a month, someone drives me a couple of hours to deliver lectures to groups at government agencies and a university.

And, of course, I plan some relaxation time at the local seniors' indoor pool where I can exercise and sit and read.

Well, this is the life that I choose. I am delighted to embrace every single day.

What will your life be like, both originally in Retirement, and your backups?

CHAPTER 18

Navigating Retirement

- ☐ Loneliness – Socialization Needs
- ☐ A Plan to say, "Goodbye"
- ☐ Practical Residence Choices
- ☐ Where is Best to Relocate?
- ☐ Staying in our home – Home Adaptation
- ☐ Working again once Retired
- ☐ Life Long Learning
- ☐ Sage Wisdom

NOW I WOULD like to address a few additional concerns that some Retirees have shared with me. I hope that you will find these ideas helpful.

Things we ALL encounter

Loneliness – Socialization Needs

- Friends from work often fade

  This is just a reality of work life. To this fear, I would say the following:

  A friend who is a friend, only at work – the relationship is unlikely to survive your departure.

  However, friendships that have more connections (live in the same neighborhood, attend the same church, go to the same gym with regularity, children are in the same schools as ours, and so forth) are far more likely to survive as friendships post-Retirement.

- Decide to meet new people – surround yourself with others, per your own needs and personality

- You WILL adapt – we all do, so relax

- Watch for the signs of Depression

  This is a serious caution. The onset of Depression is not unusual at all after a brief period of Retirement. I think this is why:

All throughout our lives, we have experienced many changes. It has been constant for the most part.

And there has been one thing that was a part of every single change event in our lives: Fear. Yes, this has always been an ingredient of changes, and quite understandably.

All changes have involved moving from a place in life that is a known, to a place that is unfamiliar. And, <u>herein lies the fear</u>. It is natural and occurs, in differing doses, for all of us.

As for Retirement, I have witnessed many times when a Retiree has been celebrated with a Retirement Party on a Friday and by the following Tuesday they have called their old boss to ask if their job is still available.

This happens because the first Monday morning in their adult life that they do not need to arise at the usual time, go through their rituals to get out the door, travel to the workplace, and be on time – this new reality is shocking – even though we have intellectually prepared for this. But the reality now sets in and it is so different that it is easy to panic and ask to be let back in.

But please don't be fooled by this natural scenario. First, know that it has happened to many before you and will happen again for most who follow you into Retirement.

Still, it will serve you well to know the warning signs of Depression and report them to your physician should they occur for you. Most people do not need any more than a mild and short-term medication. In fact, most can conquer their Depression with simple Relaxation Methods.

But, here are the classic signs in your behavior to watch for to indicate that you just might be entering a period of mild Depression:

The generally recognized signs of possible onset of Depression include: Change in eating habits, sleeping habits, sadness, feelings that there is "no end in sight" about current life problems, and the like. The best advice that I can give to you is to visit with your physician and he or she will know if you need to be referred to a Psychologist for help. Most importantly, remember that the majority of the above listed observations can have a variety of causes, but they should not be dismissed as unimportant. Depression does occur among Retirees, though it is usually quite manageable.

A Plan to say, "Goodbye"

I believe that it is a part of our human nature to seek closure and dignity in all our affairs. Leaving a job and organization of colleagues is a unique occurrence that most of us have only experienced a few times in our adult life.

When I Retired from the Fortune 100 company where I was a Vice President, I was leaving during the recovery from an illness (heart failure) that had strongly influenced my decision to Retire at that point in my life. The fact was that I did not physically return to the office. I was Retired on paper, mostly over the phone. My personal belongings were gathered from my office by someone and shipped to my home.

This left me feeling incomplete on a human level. I wanted to say goodbye to those who worked with me and for me. So, when a Retirement Party was offered I agreed wholeheartedly.

This was my opportunity to say, "Thank you" to all who had supported our common goals and to recognize that my successes were not solo accomplishments. I shook every fellow employee's hand and wished them the very best for the balance of their career and life.

This was very satisfying and I felt closure.

I know that this does not work for everyone. There are those that I have known who, when they Retired, simply cleaned out their office after hours and were missing the following work day.

I do not wish to judge or criticize this method. I believe that people are entitled to their comfort levels and to leave without fanfare is as valid an exit as mine.

Still, to most I recommend giving thought to the exit that will be the most comfortable and memorable to your personality.

At the least, I would recommend giving some thought to who on your team and within your organization you would most want to say, "Good bye" and "Thank you". Make a list of who these folks are and, at the least, send a hand-written message to each, even my internal mail. (no, I don't think that this is best done by email – it may just be my bias, but I don't feel that this is a classy or sincere format – just my bias)

Practical Residence Choices

In the not too distant past, over 50% of Retirees relocated for the years of their leisure. But, a recent survey by AARP (American Association of Retired People) found that the number of relocating Retirees is now down to about 37%.

This does not surprise me. As costs have increased and the spending of our Retirement incomes has become riskier, many of us have decided to hunker down and stay in our current homes.

Several of my Retired friends have made just this decision. They shared with me that they are familiar with and like their current home and neighborhood. Plus, in the two closest of my friends, they had both paid off their current homes and saw no good reason to collect some cash equity just to take a risk on a new venture.

I well understand my friends' thinking, although I made a different choice myself.

Still, there is a caution that I imparted to my homesteading friends. See "Home Adaptation", below.

And, if you opt to relocate, I would offer this advice:

1. Stay put for the first year (too stressful)

    A lot goes on to get accustomed to the Retirement life – fix-up projects that have been put off for years, starting hobbies, visiting and traveling to places on your "bucket list", and so forth.

2. Rent your house out and "try out" new location for 6-12 mos.

    I recommend that you not purchase a home in the first year of Retirement. This is because, if you have never lived in the geographic location to which you desire to live now, <u>you don't really know</u> that you will be happy with all the amenities and conditions of the new location. You are just assuming and too many before you have made the mistake of relocating and purchasing a new home only to find that they are just not happy in the new location. It did not live up to their dream about the location. And, yet, they are now stuck with their decision and must wait for the Real Estate sales cycles to allow them to sell and, maybe, break even.

So, try to rent a home in the new location – for at least one year if you can, while, ideally, renting out your current house. Why a year? Well, within a year, all four seasons will go by for you to see each and how satisfied you are with living there.

If, after the fourth season has gone by, you and your partner are as pleased with the location as you had dreamed, then I would say, go ahead and buy a home and sell your previous one.

3. Nearness to Family is ONE factor that attracts Retirees, but…

Suppose they move?

I have seen this happen. Some friends of mine decided, shortly after they had both Retired from their careers, to relocate to far northern New York state, to be near to their son, daughter-in-law, and grandchildren.

They sold their home in the Virginia suburbs of Washington, DC and bought a beautiful new home located about two city blocks from their family. And, all was well for about nine months. But, at that point, their daughter-in-law was offered a management promotion by her mega company employer, but it required a relocation to the West Coast.

The employer paid for the young family to sell and buy homes and they left town – leaving their loving parents in a town where they knew no one and really did not care for. Yes, they were stuck.

Presumptive babysitter?

This is a very common miscalculation that my peers have made. I mean that once Retired, whether relocating or not, they have been pressed into service by adult children to become babysitters of choice (free babysitters). In fact, one married couple with whom I have been friends most of my life, are now passing the markers for being "babysitters" and they are providing "day care" for several grandchildren and assorted nieces and nephews.

This happened incrementally, of course, not all at once. But with the addition of each child they now feel quite stuck and looking to extricate themselves from what started out as a favorable gesture and now consumes the bulk of their Retired day.

Here's my recommendation for avoiding this outcome, if you so choose. Talk to each other! As partners must throughout life. Make agreements with each other about babysitting availabilities PRIOR to Retirement and announce your boundaries to your children. Make sure that you are both (partners) on the same page on this point and communicate this to your children with a united front.

Is this foolproof? Of course not. But this is the best approach to ensure an adult-adult conversation that will be understood, appreciated, and complied with.

Where is Best to Relocate?

Making this decision is not easy. Hopefully, we give this thought over many years prior to Retirement.

We will pay attention to information that we can learn from friends and relatives as well as from the Internet.

I recommend the web site www.InternationalLiving.com as a great resource to think about becoming an expatriate and, perhaps, living full or part time in another country.

Also, if you hear of a location that trusted friends have found, you might want to plan a few long weekend trips to that location and learn about the many benefits and challenges that the location presents. And here is a listing of items, from an AARP study of members who had relocated after Retirement. The study asked the relocators to share what factors were the most important to them as they considered locations to which they might move. Here is the top of the list:

<u>Some Factors that many relocators Consider</u>

1. Within 30 minutes of good healthcare
2. Security (#1 concern for 75+)
3. Economic Opportunity
4. Public Transportation
5. People are there with common interests (min. = 3)
6. Mental Stimulation
7. Community Continuing Care (graduated care available)
8. Non-profit communities are best
9. Can you get your initial investment back if you leave?

Staying in our home – Home Adaptation

- Is someone following the taking of medications?
- Is someone (trusted) keeping an eye on spending?
- **After age 55, <u>one-floor living</u> is a better and better alternative**
- AARP offers helpful information and a complete checklist (on their website, click on "Home Adaptation")

Working again once Retired

Suppose I want to work again?

First, if you're going to get another full-time job, you're NOT Retiring, but there are other alternatives to consider.

Some choices:

- Part time Employment
- Entrepreneurial Adventures
- Second Careers (Encore)
- Stay within Government, perhaps another Agency?
- Will my age matter? (A little, but health is far more of a determinant for the employer)
- Can I keep my clearance? (If you hold a clearance, check with your local Security Officer for the rules that apply once you leave the employer. These vary, so ask BEFORE your last day. They are not allowed to discuss this with you after you are off the payroll, in most cases.)
- Best source of "networking" = those who recently left before us, USAJobs.com (for Federal Government jobs), INDEED.com (for private sector)
- Consider "Career Assessment Testing" (www. LiveCareer.com)

Career Assessment Testing is something that I recommend to all who are reentering the job market. These instruments are highly refined today and can give us data about ourselves that recommend the kinds of jobs that we will be most happy and satisfied doing. A low cost and net-based source for these telling tests can be found at the web site that I listed above.

Life Long Learning

- **Lots of resources for Seniors at Universities and Community College**

Did you know that MOST Community Colleges and MANY Universities will waive tuition for enrollees after certain chronological ages? Yes. In my state, the Community College System waives tuition for any one age 60 (that's ALL) and above. Class fees and books must still be paid, but what a DEAL!

But I have found that <u>you have to ask for the waiver</u> in order to get it.

I have taken several courses now at my local Community College and I plan to take more for as long as I am able to learn (many years, I do hope!).

Sage Wisdom

"GROWING OLD IS NOT FOR SISSIES!"
Bette Davis, Actress (1908 – 1989)

One of my favorite actresses of all time was Bette Davis.

In the year that she died, her last public appearance was on the *Johnny Carson Show*. I happened to see that show and I saw Johnny ask her if she had any words of wisdom for folks that might be watching to remember as they age.

She unhesitatingly said, "You tell them that growing old is not for sissies!"

Wow. That sage advice has stuck with me for all these years.

And now, as I enter my seventies, I really know what she meant.

But, I would add one thought to her admonition:

We have a choice. As we age we can choose to either see our aging process as a curse (many do) or as simply a change to be enjoyed – even appreciated.

After all, it's like my father used to say, "Well, this is a good day because I am on the correct side of the soil!"

In any event, I have made the choice to see every change in my physical self (the aches and body noises and the things that I used to be able to do but cannot any longer – like stand or sit easily) as a fact of living. It's all part of the drama of life and neither good nor bad, right nor wrong. It simply is.

But, in addition, I have decided to see all of life's changes with the humor that they contain. Yes. I make it a point to Laugh Out Loud – every single day – mostly at myself and the changes that I experience. They are, to me, funny – because I CHOOSE to see them that way.

In the end, my life's motto remains: ***Carpe Diem*** ("Seize The Day"). I choose to welcome every single day and relish the things that occur in the day. I look forward to tomorrow, though perhaps it may not come.

A Buddhists concept is, "Mindfulness" which is a way of enjoying every minute of every day of life by, well, "Paying Attention". I choose to NOTICE all that swirls around. When I sit on my deck, I look to see what Nature allows into my line of sight. I feel and smell and desire to just be aware of everything in my field of life.

I wish the same for you. And, so, please read the last chapter carefully. It contains the key to Happiness.

CHAPTER 19

A Final Note: Appreciating Your World-The Key to Happiness

☐ Are you appreciating the day today?

☐ Are you allowing yourself to enjoy the world around you?

☐ Even amid this dramatic change in your life, can you detach long enough to appreciate your life, the unimportant things along with the big?

☐ Are you really and genuinely enjoying every single day of life?

Practice Appreciation Every Day

So many of us wrestle with the definition of happiness. All of us seek to be happy. Of course, we do. That, in the end, is our truly common denominator. Our desire to become happy is what makes us all equal on a profound level.

I have wondered why, however, some people just seem to be happier than others. I cannot account for the disparity by simply looking at the exterior. It sure doesn't seem to be simply about "stuff" or advantageous circumstances.

A Farmer's Story

Over forty years ago, I was in the military and stationed overseas. For many months, I was stationed on the island of Okinawa.

During this time, I was not comfortable living on the base and, as an officer, I had a choice. So, I decided to live in the local village.

What a terrific opportunity to really learn about the people and their culture!

Since I had the great fortune to meet many wonderful people in the village, I was also invited to meet some of their relatives who lived in the country. One such visit was the opportunity for me to learn an important lesson about happiness.

I went to the farm of my friend's uncle. He had several acres, mostly rice paddies, and a small house, numerous chickens, two cows and a bull.

As we had arrived in the late afternoon, the uncle was able to join us, offering us rice wine as we sat down. We had not been talking for very long when I realized that I was becoming ill partly from the strong wine but also from a very overpowering stench that I had been trying to ignore since I had arrived.

When they realized that I was feeling so ill, they asked what was wrong. I replied with a question to the uncle. "What the heck is that odor?" The uncle, with a concerned look, replied, "What odor?"

I described what I smelled and how sick it was making me feel. The uncle smiled with a very knowing look. He began to speak quickly, so I had to rely on my friend's translation.

The uncle explained, "Oh, that is the smell of the manure from the livestock. It is quite natural, you know. I am glad that you mentioned this because there is something that I would like for you to know.

"Americans live in a land of amazing abundance. You have become spoiled. But more importantly, you have failed to appreciate the bounty and your good fortune. It really is a shame.

"Sure, I have animals here that create manure. But this country is not very modern. What we have seems old-fashioned to someone like you. But what I see when I look around me here are the things that allow my family to live in relative comfort, to eat, grow and thrive.

"When you smell the manure, you are revolted. When I smell it, I rejoice! It is regrettable that you only smell the manure. I smell the treasures of life and happiness."

With that he smiled broadly. He slapped my back to let me know that there were no hard feelings. And he poured more wine. The smell subsided.

Michael Townshend

The Moral

The point that he made has stuck with me all these years. The only difference between the two of us was our sense of appreciation. He had it. I lacked it. Since that time in Okinawa, I have tried to always apply this invaluable lesson.

It seems to me that all of us take so much for granted. We let time pass, and fail to revel in the wonder of the world that surrounds us.

If I spend my time worrying about things, I miss the chance to admire the glorious blue sky bathing me in sunlight, or to listen to children laughing with delight as they play together. We miss so much beauty and joy when we allow ourselves to get bogged down in events that are insignificant in the grand scheme of things.

This brings me back to the question of what constitutes happiness. If it is not found in possessions and circumstances, then what is it?

I believe happiness is determined by our attitude and approach to life. Do we focus on the Positive or the Negative?

Our faces down; steeped in worry, this does not make us happy and does not change anything. Why bother, then?

Is this the human condition? My answer is, No.

Try to think of your focus as a magnet. Whatever you focus on, you draw to your life. So, if you continually center your attention on your problems, you attract more of the same. On the other hand, if you seek to find the best in everyone and everything, you become a magnet to draw fulfillment and pleasure to your life.

What is your feeling today? Are you appreciating the day today? Are you allowing yourself to enjoy the world around you? Even amid struggles, can you stop worrying about your troubles long enough to appreciate your life, the little things along with the big?

A Final Exercise

If you would like to improve the feelings that are causing you such anguish right now or you would just simply like to feel better, here's my bottom line. Starting with this very day, *Change How You Live.*

Before this day is out, do the following:

- Do something for your Mind. Well, I guess that, by reading this book, you've already accomplished that strategy for today. *Congratulations!*
- Do something for your Body. This could be anything you would not otherwise have done. Walk up and down the staircase five times, slowly. Or just stretch

your muscles. Go for a stroll. This will be good for your body and soul.

- Do something for your Spirit. If you go on that walk, take someone with you who has not spent time with you in a while. Tell them how you feel about them; ask them to tell you all about their day. Listen patiently. You will be closer to that person, and you will have done something for someone else that really counts.
- Appreciate your world every day, every moment. Take out a pen and paper when you return home and write down five things that happened today that you really *appreciate*. You will notice your mood brighten and hope soar.

Do these things today. You will feel like, and be, a better person. You will truly be *Living Well* even in this time of Change.

BIBLIOGRAPHY

The Lotus Sutra. Translated by Burton Watson. New York: Columbia University Press, 1993.

Kubler-Ross, Elisabeth. *On Death and Dying.* New York: Macmillan and Company, 1969.

Frankl, Viktor Emil. *Man's Search for Meaning.* Boston: Beacon Press, 1962.

The Merriam-Webster New Collegiate Dictionary. Springfield, Massachusetts: Merriam-Webster, 1999.

French, Howard. "The Pretenders," *The New York Times Magazine,* p. 86-88, December 3, 2000.

Cousins, Norman. *Anatomy of an Illness as Perceived by the Patient.* New York: Norton, 1979.

Peale, Norman Vincent. *The Power of Positive Thinking.* New York: Prentice Hall, 1956.

The Writings of Nichiren Daishonin. Tokyo: Soka Gakkai Press, 1999.

Printed in the United States
By Bookmasters